온에어인터뷰

ONAIR INTERVIEW

온에어인터뷰

ONAIR INTERVIEW

김원희 지음

생각나눔

15년간 승무원으로 오대양 육대주를 내 집처럼 다니던 경험과 함께 이제는 이전의 나처럼 이 직업을 꿈꾸는 Dreamer들의 간절한 꿈을 성취하도록 도움을 주는 교육현장에서 보람 있는 시간을 보내고 있다. 많은 승무원 Dreamer들의 고민을 상담할 때면 항상 받는 질문이 있다. "너무나 외항사 승무원이 되고 싶은데 제 영어실력으로 될 수 있을까요…? 영어공부 어떻게 해야 하나요? 영어 얼마만큼 잘해야 해요?"이다. 공통점은 모두 영어의 어려움이라는 것이다

이 모든 질문의 답은 명쾌하다. 항공사 승무원이 되기 위해 통과해야 하는 영어면접은 면접을 위한 영어를 준비하는 것이지, 영어 자체의 능력을 평가받는 것이 아니라는 것이다. 출발 선상에서 이러한 생각의 전환은 큰 변화를 가져온다. 인터뷰 준비 전에 온통 영어! 영어! 영어에 기죽어 발도 떼어 보지 못하는 수많은 Cabin Crew Dreamer들이 있기 때문이다. 인터뷰 즉 면접이라는 것은 결국 나에 대한 것을 면접관에게 알려 주는 것이기 때문에 질문의 패턴과 답변은 생각 이상으로 쉽고 반복적이며, 이것은 100문 100답이라

는 것을 완성했을 때 학생들 본인도 모르게 자연스럽게 입을 벌려 말을 하는 모습을 발견하며 놀라게 될 것이다. 이것이 인터뷰 영어의 비밀이다. (The Secret of Interview-English.)

이러한 취지에서 100문 100답의 선행과제를 해결하는 것은 외항사를 준비하는 데 있어서 최우선으로 해결해야 하는 점이다. 그러나 이러한 체계가 잡히기 전에 면접탈락으로 낙심하거나 현실적으로 직장을 다녀서 시간이 없는 경우, 또는 다른 개인적인 사정으로 이른바 학원에 다닐 수 없어서 준비를 차일피일 미루게 되는 경우, 때로는 지나친 영어 자체 skill(문법, 회화, 토익 등)을 업그레이드하는 데 집착하며, 지쳐서 결국 꿈을 버리게 되는 많은 경우를 본인은 교육 현장에서 보아 왔다. 그래서 이것을 해결할 방법을 찾고 고민하다가 만들게 된 것이 바로 외항사 최초 인터넷 강의 사이트인 On Air Interview의 창업 모티브이다. (www.onairinterview.com)

On Air Interview 교재는 해설이 없이 순전히 질문과 답변 위주로 되어 있으며 각 샘플 답변 밑에는 자신의 답변을 완성하여 답변

준비 노트로 활용할 수 있도록 만들어져 있어 답변 준비에 집중할 수 있도록 만들어져 있다. 이 교재 한권만으로도 마지막 장의 답변을 완성하는 순간 항공사 영어 인터뷰의 자신감을 갖게 될 것이다.

마지막 당부의 말

Just do it!

어느 유명한 스포츠 용품의 광고 카피이다. 이것은 승무원을 꿈꾸며 준비했던 그 때나 지금이나 나의 최고의 인생 모토이다. 모든 것을 너무나 많이 생각하고 고민한다면 인생에서 얻을 수 있는 것은 결코 없을 것이다. You tube의 창업자인 스티브 첸 또한 행하는 Dreamer 를 강조하고 있고 그것이 유투브 창업의 모토임을 밝히고 있다.

본인도 영어가 절대적으로 부족한 상태에서 3개월이라는 기적의 시간을 보내고 당당히 케세이퍼시픽을 입사했던 자로서 그 방법을 제시하며 '영어 때문에 못해요' 라는 말이 얼마나 무색한 변명인지를 지난 3년간의 많은 합격자를 통해 또한 입증하고 있다. 요즘엔 많은 외항사들이 결혼과 상관없이 나이와 상관없이(36-40살의 합격자) 승무원을 채용하고 있으며 실제로 많은 Dreamer들이 결혼하고 아이가 있음에도 도전하는 것을 보고 있다. 36살의 합격자 또한 최근에 나오고 있다. 지금 꿈꾸고 있다면 주저하지 마라! 단지 지금 시작하라! 지금 시작하면 1년 후 오늘 당신은 하늘을 날고 있을 것이기 때문에….

　그리고 승무원이라는 일은 주저하며 시간을 보내기엔 너무 아까운 직업이기 때문에….

To all cabin crew Dreamer

From Lucia W.H Kim the C.E.O of OnAir Interview

| CONTENTS |

승무원 영어면접
핵심 답변

• 온에어 인터뷰 •

ONAIR
INTERVIEW

영어면접 핵심 답변 개념 잡기!
'지피지기면 백전불패'

"If you know yourself you win 50 battles out of a hundred.

If you know your enemy you win 50.

But if you know yourself and your enemy you win hundred

battles out of a hundred."

—Sun Tzu's Art of War—

	Subject	Why for Interviewer / 왜 면접관이 물어보는지…
1	면접 개요	최고의 서비스직이라 불리는 승무원 면접에서 서 있을 때와 앉아 있을 때의 자세, 어법, 미소와 인사 매너 등은 기본이지만 중요한 평가 대상이 된다. 주의사항과 함께 평소에 꾸준히 연습하여 몸에 배게 해야 한다.

Why for myself / 나의 답변 접근 핵심정리

	Subject	Why for Interviewer / 왜 면접관이 물어보는지…
2	Small talk	Ice break! 즉, 면접관이 면접자의 긴장감과 어색함을 풀어주기 위한 것, 이것은 인터뷰를 여는 문의 역할을 하는 것이다. 면접자도 적극적으로 면접관과 친밀감 형성을 위해 긴장을 풀고 마음을 열어야 한다. 기내에서도 승무원의 duty 중의 하나가 승객과 small talk를 하는 것이기 때문에 면접관들은 긴장을 풀어줌과 동시에 small talk를 통해 승무원의 자질을 엿보려고 한다. 따라서 짧은 질문과 답이지만 면접자들은 긍정의 에너지로, 특히 첫 인사말은 밝고 적극적으로 인사하도록 하자.

Why for myself / 나의 답변 접근 핵심정리

	Subject	Why for Interviewer / 왜 면접관이 물어보는지…
3	Personal data	개인의 신상명세 파악이 목적, 간결하게 면접관이 알고자 하는 사항을 전달한다.

Why for myself / 나의 답변 접근 핵심정리

	Subject	Why for Interviewer / 왜 면접관이 물어보는지…
4	Personality	승무원직업의 성격과 면접자의 성격이 맞는지의 여부를 판단하기 위한 것이다. 승무원직업의 성격이란 1) 많은 사람을 만나야 한다. 2) 활동성, 즉 한곳에 머무르지 않고 다양한 장소를 이동하며 일한다. 3) 서비스를 한다. 등이 있다. 이런 성격의 직업을 수행하기 위해서는 1) friendly, cheerful, open-minded, sociable, outgoing 등 2) active, adaptable, adventurous, global mindset, enthusiastic 등 3) service mind, calm, flexible, generous, reliable 등의 성격이 본인에게 있음을 말해주어야 한다.

상대적으로 너무 내성적이거나 감정적, 정적인 성격의 어필은 위험하다.

	Subject	Why for Interviewer / 왜 면접관이 물어보는지…
5	Hobby	취미란 본인이 즐기고 좋아하는 일을 여가 시간에 하는 것이므로 취미에 관련한 질문은 그 사람의 성향과 적성을 파악하는 좋은 방법이다. 성격 질문과도 연결되는 질문이며 독서, 음악감상 등의 너무 정적인 취미 보다는 승무원직업의 특성과 적합한 활동적이고 여러 사람이 함께할 수 있는 답변을 준비하자.

똑같은 취미도 어떻게 답을 하느냐에 따라 임팩트를 주거나 식상한 대답이 될 수 있다. 예를 들면, 첼로가 취미인 A 학생은 취미는 첼로이다라고 하며 답변을 마무리 한 경우와 B 학생은 첼로가 취미이고 한 달에 한 번은 오케스트라 단원을 만나 협연을 한다. 그것을 통해 team work를 배운다고 마무리했을 때 분명히 A와 B가 주는 임팩트는 큰 차이를 준다. 이렇듯 많은 사람과 어울리고 활동적인 취미로 대답하는 것이 key point라고 할 수 있다.

Why for myself / 나의 답변 접근 핵심정리

	Subject	Why for Interviewer / 왜 면접관이 물어보는지…
6	Health care	승무원의 자질에서 중요한 것 중의 하나는 건강이다. 시차 극복과 불규칙한 생활은 승무원직업의 어려운 점 중의 하나이며, 건강하지 않을 경우 할 수 없는 직업 또한 승무원이다. 따라서 높은 자기관리 능력이 요구되며 평소 꾸준히 건강에 관심을 갖고 관리의 습관이 형성되어 있는 후보자를 선호한다. 이렇듯 면접관(특별히 더 외국항공사)들은 이목구비가 예쁜 후보자보다는 건강한 에너지를 전달하는 면접자를 선호한다. 면접의 합격뿐만 아니라 성공적인 cabin crew- life를 보내기 위해서는 건강은 필수조건이다. 오늘부터 당장 실천에 옮기며 면접을 준비하도록 한다.

Why for myself / 나의 답변 접근 핵심정리

	Subject	Why for Interviewer / 왜 면접관이 물어보는지…
7	School life	학생이거나 졸업한 지 1년 미만이 학생들은 상대적으로 사회경험이 많지 않기 때문에 면접관들은 그들의 학교생활과 경험을 통해 social skill이나 team work skill이 있는지, 그리고 성숙한 인성으로 승객을 응대할 수 있는 다른 skill들이 있는지를 파악하게 된다. 따라서 답변을 준비할 때에 이점을 충분히 염두에 두고 답변의 내용을 완성해야 하는데, 가령 예를 들면 독어독문이 전공인 A 학생은 자신의 전공 소개에서 독일의 유명한 소설가 헤르만 헤세를 말하며 그 소설책을 읽고 감명을 받았다는 식의 내용만을 말했고, B는 독어독문 전공인데 그것을 통해 독일어로 말하고 읽는 법도 배웠다. 그래서 기내에서 독일어로 기내 방송하는 것이 자신 있다는 식으로 했을 때 B에게 더 점수를 줌에는 틀림이 없을 것이다.

Why for myself / 나의 답변 접근 핵심정리

	Subject	Why for Interviewer / 왜 면접관이 물어보는지…
8	Work experience	면접관이 왜 나의 전 직장에 관심이 있을까? 이런 식의 생각 접근은 매우 중요하다. 승무원 직과 관련이 없는 연구직이나 다른 기타 경력자는 전 직장에 대해 더 심도 있게 질문을 받는 경우를 많이 본다. 왜일까? 왜냐하면, 업무 성격이 다른 승무원이라는 특수 서비스직을 이행할 수 있는 여지가 있는지를 알아보기 위함이다. 따라서 면접자들은 전 직장 관련 질문을 철저히 준비하고 다른 성격의 업무였을수록 승무원으로의 이직의 이유를 승무원이 되고자 하는 열정과 함께 준비되어있음을 확실히 보여주어야 한다.

Why for myself / 나의 답변 접근 핵심정리

	Subject	Why for Interviewer / 왜 면접관이 물어보는지…
9	Overseas Experience	승무원 직의 적성, 즉 Aptitude를 알아보는 최적의 질문이 Hobby와 함께 Overseas Experience이다. 특히, 외항사는 항상 함께 일하는 팀 동료뿐만 아니라 서비스해야 하는 대상이 외국인이므로, 외국에 오랫동안 체류한 경험이라든지 여행 경험을 소지한 면접자를 선호할 수밖에 없다. 그러나 외국여행경험이 없다 하더라도 이것이 탈락의 원인이 될 수는 없으며, 그것을 극복하기 위한 노력을 어떻게 해왔고 세계관을 갖고 있는 사람임을 어필한다면 문제가 없다.

Why for myself / 나의 답변 접근 핵심정리

	Subject	
10	Self-introduction	자기소개는 말 그대로 나를 내가 표현하는 것이므로 정형화된 형식은 없다. 그러나 합격을 위한 자기소개는 내가 하고 싶은 자기소개가 아닌 면접관이 듣고 싶어하는 자기소개이다. 　보통은 생각의 흐름을 따라가는 것이 좋으며, 이때 생각의 흐름이란 일반적으로 모든 사람이 낯선 누군가를 처음 만났을 때 상대방에게 궁금하게 생각하는 것의 흐름을 따라가면 가장 좋다. 흔한 예로 미팅하는 장면을 머리에 그리며 상대방에게 궁금한 것은 무엇인지 생각해본다면, 이 답은 의외로 쉽게 정리될 것이다.

Why for myself / 나의 답변 접근 핵심정리

	Subject	Why for Interviewer / 왜 면접관이 물어보는지…
11	Job of F/A	승무원이 너무 되고 싶다고 하면서 막상 승무원 일에 대해 질문했을 때 핵심적이고 구체적인 key word가 면접자의 답에서 나오지 않는다면 면접관은 실망하게 된다. 그 직업의 열정은 관심도와 일치한다고 본다. 직업의 관심도는 직업에 대한 구체적인 지식을 갖고 있다는 것을 보여 줄 수 있어야 한다.

Why for myself / 나의 답변 접근 핵심정리

	Subject	Why for Interviewer / 왜 면접관이 물어보는지…
12	Why do you want to be a F/A?	왜 승무원이 되고자 하는지 지원 동기를 물어본다. 기업에서는 그 일에 대한 열정과 애정으로 진심으로 일할 수 있는 직원을 찾는다.

간혹 자질만 얘기하는 경우, 즉 예를 들면 "난 잘 웃고 사교성도 좋고 영어를 잘해, 그래서 승무원이 하고 싶어."라고 한다면, 이것은 본인의 순수한 하고 싶은 이유가 아니라 자질을 어필하면서 열정은 없어 보이고 핵심을 찌르지 못하는 답이 될 수 있다.

본인의 마음을 들여다보고 그 안의 열정이라는 보석을 꺼내도록 해보자!

Why for myself / 나의 답변 접근 핵심정리

	Subject	Why for Interviewer / 왜 면접관이 물어보는지…
13	Why should we hire you?	이 질문은 다른 말로 표현한다면 "너의 자질을 한번 내게 어필 해봐."이다.

이런 질문을 받을 때야말로 자신 있게 본인이 갖고 있는 승무원 일에 적합한 자질과 특기를 열심히 답해야 한다.

Why for myself / 나의 답변 접근 핵심정리

	Subject	Why for Interviewer / 왜 면접관이 물어보는지…
14	Visions/ Aspiration	왜 면접관이 나의 비전과 향후 미래의 모습을 궁금해할까? 물론 면접자 삶의 계획과 열정을 통한 그 사람의 태도를 보고자 하는 것도 있으나, 항공사는 이 면접자가 우리 항공사에 입사하면 얼마나 오래 일할 것인지에 관심이 더 있다. 한 명의 승무원을 모집하여 교육을 시키는 것은 많은 비용이 투자되기 때문에 단기간 일하려는 면접자는 같은 조건에서는 잘 뽑지 않으려 할 것이다.

	Subject	Why for Interviewer / 왜 면접관이 물어보는지…
15	In flight situation –Service	기내상황의 대처능력을 통해 면접자의 자질을 파악함과 동시에 업무수행능력을 보기 위함이다. 순발력을 요구하는 질문부터 좀 더 전문적인 지식의 수준까지 요구하는 경우가 있어 체계적으로 준비해야 한다. Service는 크게 Anticipating 할 수 있는 자질 테스트 Complaining 처리 능력으로 질문한다.

Why for myself / 나의 답변 접근 핵심정리

	Subject	Why for Interviewer / 왜 면접관이 물어보는지…
16	In flight situation –Safety	안전에 관련된 기내상황질문은 정확한 답변도 중요하나, 면접관은 면접자들이 안전에 타협하지 않는 마음자세를 갖고 있는지를 측정하는 것이 주목적이다.
Why for myself / 나의 답변 접근 핵심정리		

	Subject	Why for Interviewer / 왜 면접관이 물어보는지…
17	In flight situation –Team work	외국항공사의 독특한 근무 환경에서 발생할 수 있는 상황에 대한 순발력을 보여주어야 하고 그 때 표현하면 좋은 key word로 준비한다.

Why for myself / 나의 답변 접근 핵심정리

	Subject	Why for Interviewer / 왜 면접관이 물어보는지…
18	In flight situation –etc	기타상황은 너무 심각하게 대처하기보다는 주로 순발력과 재치 있는 답변을 요구하는 경우가 많다.

Why for myself / 나의 답변 접근 핵심정리

Interview란?

1. 면접 개념

회사에 입사하기 위해 면접관과 얼굴을 맞대어 회사에 적합한 자질을 테스트받는 과정이다. INTERVIEW에 합격하기 위해서는 interview라는 용어의 개념에 대해 파악해야 할 필요가 있으며, 이것은 합격을 위한 핵심 답변작성에 매우 중요한 선 과제라고 할 수 있다.

INTERVIEW라는 단어는 INTER + VIEW로 구성되어 있다.

여기서 INTER는 상호 교류를 의미하며, VIEW는 보다(SEE)의 의미이다.

즉, 면접관은 나에게 질문(QUESTION)을 주고 나는 면접관에게 답(ANSWER)을 주며, 상호작용(INTER) 속에서 면접관은 보게(VIEW) 된다. 이때 나는 면접관에게 회사의 인재상에 맞는 자질(QUALIFICATION)을 보여줘야 하며, 이것이 성공적인 면접의 핵심이다.

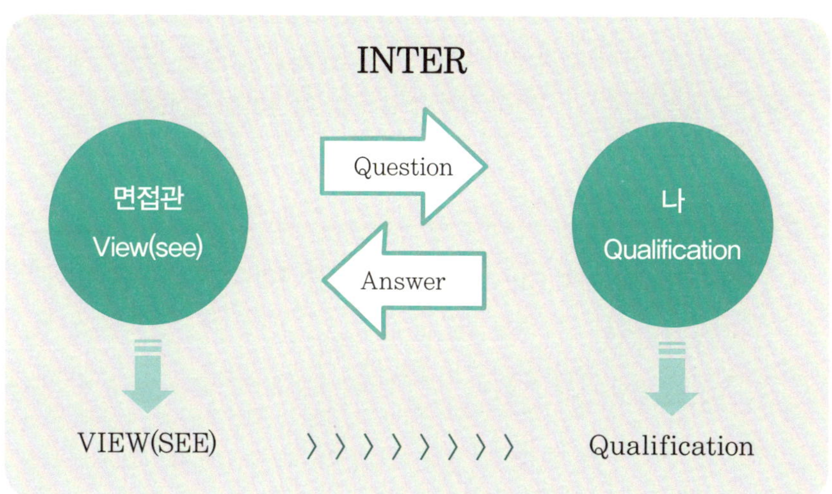

2. 합격의 조건

'면접을 합격한다'의 영어적 표현은 'PASS the INTERVIEW!'이고, 이때 PASS라는 단어에 합격을 위한 key point가 있다.

P-ersonality 승무원 직업성격에 맞는 나의 성격을 제시하여야 한다.
  ex) outgoing, friendly, open-minded

A-ptitude 승무원 직업의 적성을 알아볼 수 있는 최적의 질문은 hobby, overseas experience이다. 특히 hobby는 내가 여유있는 시간에 좋아하는 것을 즐기는 것이라고 볼 때 개인의 적성을 판단할 수 있는 최적의 질문이라고 볼 수 있으므로 승무원직의 성격과 어울리는 활동적인 취미로 하도록 한다.

S-kill 모든 직업이 그렇듯이 승무원 직업도 skill이 필요하다.
  ex) communication skill, language skill, interpersonal skill

S-mile 면접 시 긴장하며 말할 때 쓰는 얼굴 근육을 부드럽게 풀어주며 모음(a, e, i, o, u) 위주의 표정을 연습하여야 한다.

*** 외국항공사 채용절차**

1. 외국항공사 공채(OR 기관을 통한 채용대행)
2. OPEN DAY
3. ASSESSMENT DAY

1. 외국항공사 공채(OR 기관을 통한 채용대행)

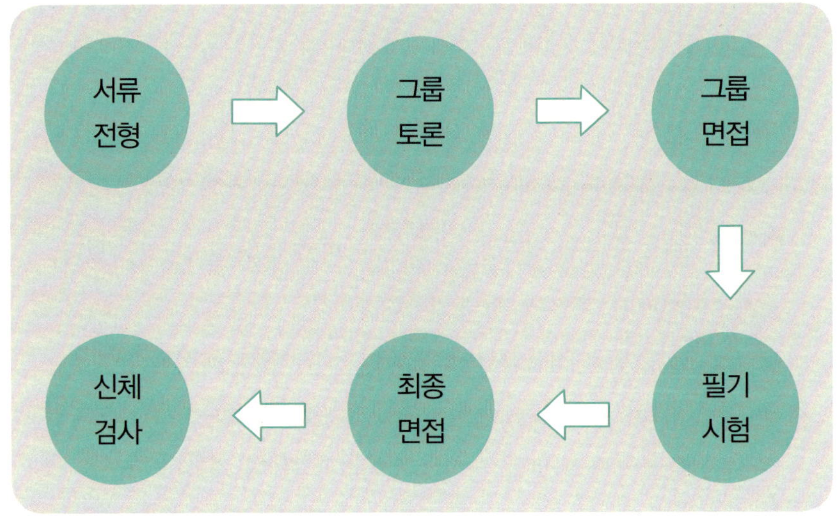

2. OPEN DAY

Open day는 지원자가 CV/RESUME 를 들고 날짜, 시간을 잡아

놓고 지정한 나라(도시)의 진행 장소로 가서 직접서류를 내고 면접 보는 형태 ★빠른 친밀감 형성 요망

  1) 준비물- CV/RESUME, 면접복장

  2) 대표 항공사- 에미레이트 항공사, 카타르 항공사

  3) 순서

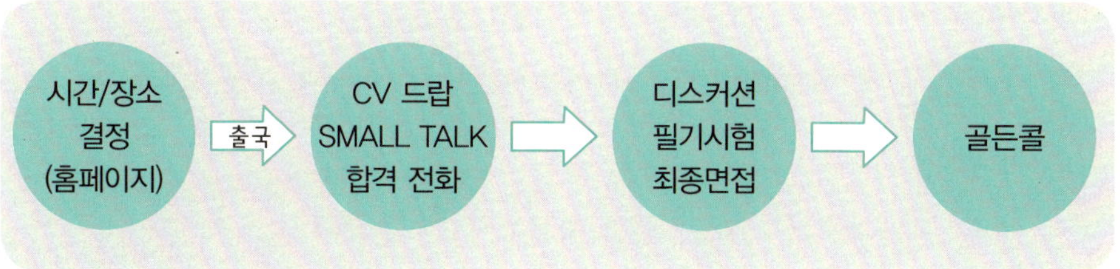

3. ASSESSMENT DAY

open day와 다르게 메일로 이력서를 보내고 합격하면 항공사에서 보내는 초대장 즉 invitation을 받고 면접장소로 출국 하게 된다.

  1) 준비물- 면접복장

  2) 대표 항공사- 에띠하드 항공사, 플라이듀바이 항공사

  3) 순서

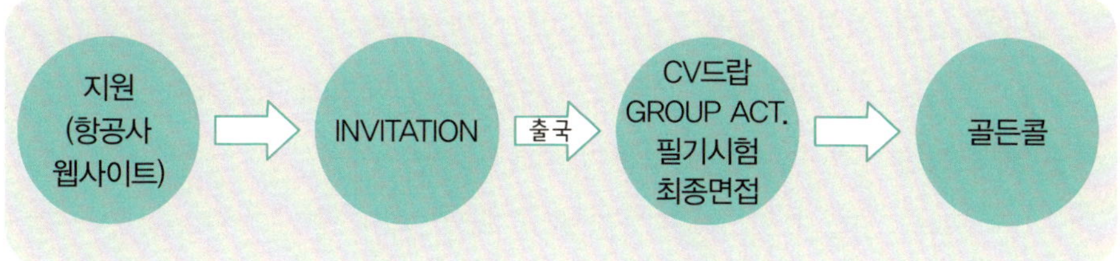

영어인터뷰

Let's start!

1) 기본 매너

면접하는 장소: 면접 보는 건물에서는 항상 언행 심사를 조심하여야 한다.

(ex. 건물 화장실, 복도, 주변 시설물 등)

대기실에서 면접은 시작: 외항사의 경우는 응시자가 많을 경우 별도의 대기실에서 기다리다가 면접실에 들어가는 경우가 많다. 웃음을 잃지 말고 준비한 내용을 잘 검토하라.

면접실 입장 전: 문 앞에서는 머리에서 발끝까지 자세를 준비해야 한다. 마음의 미소도 포함.

자신감 있게 입장하라: 대부분은 면접관이 이미 착석해 있는 경우이고, 이때 면접실에 앉아있다가 면접관이 들어오는 경우는 면접관이 들어오면 자리에서 일어나는 것이 예의이다. 이때 한국식으로 허리를 굽혀 인사하지 말고, 반듯하게 서서 eye-contact를 하며 밝은 미소를 짓는다. 먼저 악수를 청하는 것은 예의에 어긋나며 면접관이 청할 경우 가볍게 악수하면 된다.

면접관의 이름을 알아두면 유리하다: 예를 들면, 'Good Morning, sir' 하는 것보다는 'Good morning, Mr. Baker' 하는 것이 인터뷰를 더 친근감 있게 만들어 준다. 이때부터 본격적인 인터뷰에 앞서 small Talk가 오가는 것이 일반적이며, 대부분 이때 80% 이상의 호감도가 형성된다.

적극적인 인사말: 예를 들면, 'How are you?'라는 말에 'I'm fine' 이라는 말보다는 'I'm great. Thank you. How about you?'라는 대답이 더 친근하게 느껴진다.

2) 표현 매너

1. 면접실에 들어가서

간단한 인사지만 승무원의 자질이 가장 많이 나타나는 순간

위축되지 말고 자신감 있게 인사 하는 것이 중요

첫인상은 만난 지 30초 만에 결정된다.

승무원은 항상 승객에게 인사를 건네는 사람이다. 먼저 인사를 건네는 것이 좋은 인상을 줄 수 있으며, 인사를 받은 경우는 꼭 되물어 준다.

Hello. Good morning/Good afternoon/Good evening, sir

Hello. It's nice to meet you.

How are you doing, sir/ma'am?

I'm honored to be here.

I'm pleased to meet you.

I'm pleased to have been given this interview opportunity.

I'm honored to have this interview opportunity.

2. 면접관 말을 알아듣기 힘들 때

여기서는 못 알아들어도 자연스럽고 정중하게 다시 묻는 여유가
중요

Would you please say that again?

Could you repeat what you said?

I beg your pardon, sir/ma'am?

긴 문장을 듣다가 놓쳤을 때

I'm sorry but I couldn't follow that. Would you say that
again?

I'm sorry sir, but I didn't hear you. Would you mind
repeating that again?

I'm afraid that I didn't understand your question. Would
you mind saying that again?

다시 설명해줬는데도 모를 때

Sorry, I still don't get it.

여전히 못 알아들을 때

I'm not sure that I understand you.

3. 면접관 말이 너무 빠를 때

Could you speak more slowly please?

I'm sorry but I couldn't catch what you said.

I'm sorry but I couldn't follow you.

4. 영어 표현이 떠오르지 않을 때

면접 도중 실수하더라도 끝까지 최선을 다하는 태도가 중요. 대답이 떠오르지 않을 때는 "I'm sorry."라기 보다는 "Can you give me a second?"라고 말하는 게 좋다.

5. 면접관 말에 맞장구를 칠 때

남발하는 것은 좋지 않으나 적절할 때 한두 마디는 대화의 분위기에 좋은 효과를 준다.

That's right.

I think so.

I understand, is that so(right)?

6. 면접관이 Thank you 라고 했을 때

It was my pleasure.

No problem

You're welcome

Don't mention it.

Not at all/ It's nothing at all.

7. 부정적이 답변을 해야 할 경우는

I'm afraid that…that은 생략해도 된다

Ex) I am afraid that I tend to be slightly sensitive.

I am afraid that I tend to feel a strong ownership towards my work.

8. 면접이 끝났을 때

Thank you for your time. I had such a great time with you sir/ ma'am.

It has been a pleasure talking with you./ I've enjoyed talking with you.

Before I leave, I would like to thank you for meeting me today.

9. 면접관 말에 수긍할 때에는 okay라고 하지 말고 certainly 라고 한다.

3) 표정, 동작의 매너

아이컨택과 스마일: 자신감의 표현, 눈을 피하지 말고 더욱 자신 있게 눈으로도 의사소통하라.

면접관이 다수인 경우, 골고루 모든 면접관과 아이컨택을 하라.

보디랭귀지: 지나치거나 난잡한 손동작에 유의하라. 그러나 적절한 손동작은 대화를 활기 있게 만듦으로 거울을 보며 연습. 손동작을 쓸 때에는 손바닥 안이 상대방에게 보이지 않게 하며 손끝을 가지런히 모은다. 앉아있을 때의 기본자세는 어깨의 힘을 풀고 손은 가지런히 배꼽 아래에, 허리는 꼿꼿이 세워 엉덩이에 힘을 주며 무릎이 붙게 한다. 머리를 흔든다거나 손으로 얼굴을 만지는 동작에 유의한다.

목소리, 톤, 발음, 강세, 억양: 긍정적이고 자신감 있는 목소리가 중요, 실수를 해도 당당하고 겸손한 목소리로 대답하라. 우물쭈물하거나 목소리가 작지 않도록 한다. 지나치게 혀를 굴리는 등의 부자연스런 발음은 기피하라.

Small Talk

Small Talk란

Small talk is socially important in certain situations, even though it consists of meaningless conversation in terms of content. In many English-speaking countries, it is important to mingle and speak with other guests at social functions and small talk can also be used to break the ice and help guests to chat. Also, small talk helps a flight attendant in creating a warm atmosphere in-flight and is important with passengers because the company can find out if the needs of the passengers are being met or not.

1. Small Talk의 예

The appropriate small talk is mainly composed of non-personal comments about non-controversial subjects.

For example

2-1. Discussing the weather with people you don't really

know.

2-2. Engaging in conversations with people we may see every day but not know personally.

e.g people we share the elevator with in an office building but not know personally.

2-3. Complements can be a way to have small talk.

e.g one woman at a party complementing another on her dress.

2. Small Talk의 주의점(기내에서 승객에게 할 때)

When talking to passengers there are several points that you have to bear in mind.

3-1. All passengers should be treated equally regardless of their gender, race, nationality, or nature of their travel.

3-2. Use your own judgement to see if the passenger would like to be talked to e.g. do not disturb those who are eating or appear to be busy.

3-3. Do not prolong a conversation. Try to have small talk with as many passengers as possible.

3-4. Avoid a monologue

3-5. Try not to change the topic abruptly.

3-6. Avoid sensitive topics such as:

Politics/Religion/Culture/Company policy/Your grievances/

Subjects that are too personal/Disasters e.g. aircraft crashes

3. 영어인터뷰 시 Small Talk의 예

1. Can I have your name and number, please? May I have your name please?

▤ Yes, my name is 000. But you can call me 000. My application No is 000.

| 나의 답변 |

------

2. What can I call you?/ What's your English name?

▤ 1. You can call me Lucy.

▤ 2. You can call me Hae.

3. What is the meaning of your name?

1. My name is Lee Eun Hae which means Grace. My parents gave me this name, hoping my life to be full of favor and appreciation.

4. How are you today?/ How do you feel right now?/Are you ok?

1. I'm great. I'm a little nervous but I'm very excited for this interview. I feel like my dream is about to come true. How about you, sir/ma'am?

2. It couldn't be better. Today, I feel like I am one step closer to making my dream come true. How are you

today, sir/ma'am?

---

5. How's the weather today?

1. 날씨가 좋을 때

(1) The weather is great today, so I feel great as well!

(2) It's lovely! I really like sunny days and it's gorgeous outside!

2. 날씨가 나쁠 때

(1) The weather is pretty bad, but that doesn't affect me at all because I'm excited for this interview!

(2) It's pretty hot and humid outside, but I feel fine since we are indoors with air conditioning.

(3) It's very cold and raining. I hope you brought an umbrella with you./ I hope you brought your rain coat.

(4) It's snowing! It snows a lot here, but every time it snows, I'm still always amazed. It's so beautiful to look at!

- -

- -

- -

- -

---

6. Did you have (breakfast/lunch/dinner) today?/ What did you have?/ Who did you eat with?

1. Yes I did. I had rice and soup with my parents. Usually, I have breakfast with my parents. And I love this time of day because I can talk about my life and get sound advice from them.

2. Yes, I had some cereal with yogurt and some fruit for breakfast.

- -

- -

7. What time did you go to bed last night?/ Did you sleep well last night?

📧 1. I went to bed quite early to be well rested for today. And fortunately, I slept very well and now I'm in great shape physically and mentally for this interview.

📧 2. Yes, I slept very well last night and even dreamed that I was wearing your airline uniform.

| 나의 답변 |

----

8. What time did you get up this morning?

📧 1. I got up very early because I wanted to be well prepared for today, and also I could arrive here an hour and a half early.

| 나의 답변 |

9. What did you do before you came in today?

📧 1. I woke up early to get prepared for my interview and went over my notes about your company. I also tried to anticipate some of the questions, I would be asked.

---

10. What did your parents say to you this morning?

📧 1. My parents are very supportive of my dream and they wished me good luck and told me to do my best. If I pass this interview, they will be very delighted.

📧 2. They encouraged me a lot and told me to do my best. I am always thankful for my family, because they are always supporting my dream to the best of their abilities.

Personal Data

1. When were you born?/ When is your birthday?

📑 1. I was born on September 17th 1990. (My birthday is on the 17th of September). Since I was born in the fall, this is my favorite season. Especially, because I enjoy going on trips to view the autumn foliage.

| 나의 답변 |

----

2. Where were you born?/ What is your birthplace?/ Tell me about your hometown.

📑 1. I was born in Gyungju, which is famous for its historical sites of Korea. But Seoul is like my second hometown because I moved to Seoul when I was 5 years old.

📑 2. I was born near Gangnam in Seoul. I'm so proud of

my hometown because it's the capital city of Korea. Nowadays, it's getting more internationally famous since the song Gangnam style by Psy had a mega hit all over the world. I would strongly recommend you to visit Gangnam and enjoy the exciting street life.

---

3. Where do you live?

1. I live in Bundang right now, which is near Seoul. It takes about 40 minutes from here by subway. I think Bundang is quite a great place to live in because there are many parks and shopping malls. Above all, transportation is very conveniently set up there.

2. I currently live near Hongdae station in Seoul. It only takes me about half an hour from here by bus. The streets that I pass by to get here are very lively with lots of shops and a trendy neighborhood. (유행의 첨단을 걷는)

3. I live in Incheon and it took me about an hour to get here today. I had to take a bus and then switch to riding the subway to travel across town. It was a bit of a long trip.

---

4. How tall are you?

1. I am 165 centimeters tall. I'm sure I can reach the overhead lockers in an aircraft with no problem.

2. My height is 163 cm. I think my height is tall enough to work as a flight attendant.

5. Please tell me your weight.

📑 1. I weigh 50 kg. I always exercise to keep myself in good shape.

| 나의 답변 |

- -

6. What's your vision?/ What is your eyesight?

📑 1. My corrected eyesight is 1.0 for my right eye and 1.5 for my left.

📑 2. I have 1.0 eyesight on both sides.

📑 3. My right eyesight is 1.5 and my left eyesight is 1.0

| 나의 답변 |

- -

7. Please tell me about your family.

📑 1. My family has four members: my father, mother, younger sister and me.

My father has been working for a trading company for 25 years and he is a very diligent man. My mother stays at home and takes care of the house.

She is a very kind and warm-hearted person. My younger sister entered 00university this year, and is majoring in Philosophy.

I love my family so much and I appreciate them for always supporting my dream.

I hope I can fulfill their expectations by passing this interview.

4 Personality

* Personality 성격의 표현법

1. S + V + 형

I am careful with my actions. 저는 행동이 신중합니다.

I am decisive. 저는 결단력이 있습니다.

I am passionate. 저는 정열적입니다.

I am disciplined. 저는 규율을 잘 따릅니다.

I am very responsible. 저는 책임감이 굉장히 강합니다.

2. I am a person who is…

I am a person who is down-to-earth. 저는 현실적인 사람입니다.

I am a person who is resourceful. 저는 수완이 좋은 사람입니다.

I am a person who respects others. 저는 다른 사람을 존중하는 사람입니다.

I am a person who is friendly and outgoing. 저는 우호적이고 활발한 사람입니다.

3. I consider myself (to be)…

I consider myself (to be) a bit indecisive. 저는 제가 약간 우유부단하다고 생각합니다.

I consider myself (to be) enthusiastic. 저는 제가 열정이 넘친다고 생각합니다.

I consider myself (to be) quick-witted. 저는 제가 재치 있다고 생각합니다.

I consider myself (to be) flexible. 저는 제가 융통성이 있다고 생각합니다.

I consider myself to be responsible and adaptable. 저는 제 자신이 책임감 있고 적응을 잘한다고 생각합니다.

| 성격을 나타내는 형용사 |

active	활동적인, 적극적인	generous	관대한
adaptable	적응할 수 있는	hard working	열심히 일하는
calm	차분한	humble	겸손한
cheerful	발랄한	optimistic	긍정적인
diligent	근면한	open minded	마음이 열린
enthusiastic	열정이 넘치는	outgoing	외향적인
easygoing	원만한	reliable	신뢰할 수 있는
		sociable	사교적인

friendly	다정한	strong-willed	강인한
feminine	여성스러운	stoic	감정적이 아닌
flexible	관대한 융통성 있는	warm hearted	마음이 따뜻한

4. I have +명사

I have patience 저는 인내심이 있습니다.

I have a good imagination. 저는 상상력이 있습니다.

I have a global mindset. 저는 세계적인 사고 방식을 지니고 있습니다.

5. …represents who I am

I think my responsibility represents who I am 책임감은 저를 나타냅니다.

6. I have a sense of +명사

I have a sense of humor 나는 유머 감각이 있습니다.

| 성격을 나타내는 명사 |

caring heart	따뜻한 마음	people skills	사교술
creativity	창의력	responsibility	책임감

| empathy | 공감 | sympathy | 동정심 |
| leadership | 리더십 | | |

7. I like to 저는 …하기를 좋아합니다

I like to help those in need. 저는 도움이 필요한 사람들을 돕는 것을 좋아합니다.

I like to learn about new things every day. 저는 매일 새로운 것을 배우는 것을 좋아합니다.

I like to be around people. 저는 사람들과 함께 있는 것을 좋아합니다.

I like to challenge myself with new ideas. 저는 새로운 생각들로 제 자신에게 도전하는 것을 좋아합니다.

* Personality 질문 유형

Why) 기본적으로 승무원에 유리한 성격은 많은 사람과 잘 어울리는 외향적, 적극적, 사교적이며, 밝고 생기 있어 보여야 한다. 그러나 본인은 밝고 명랑하다고 하면서 표정이나 눈빛이 면접관에게 전혀 그렇게 보이지 않는다면, 오히려 감점요소가 될 수 있으므로 주의하여야 한다. 또한, 평소에 꾸준하고 규칙적인 운동을 통해 건강한 에너지를 전달할 수 있어야 한다.

1. What kind of personality do you think you have?

1. 외향적이고 활동적인 사람

I am a very outgoing and active person. I always enjoy going out and meeting lots of people. And I am very adaptable and can adjust to any kind of person or even circumstances. So in my opinion, my personality suits this job very well.

2. 친절하고 사교적인 사람

People say that I am very friendly and also a sociable person because I make them feel comfortable around me, even when I had just met them. Also, I am someone who helps people get closer together by bridging the gaps. Because of these things, I believe I will be very helpful working as a flight attendant.

3. 열정적이고 적극적인 사람

I believe I am a very positive person. When I complete a task, I always go one step ahead and am proactive in achieving my goals. This has always given me good results and this success also gives me enthusiasm to look for new goals.

📑 4. 이해심이 많고 배려하는 사람

I consider myself to be a considerate and understanding person. I always put myself into another person's shoes to understand their situations and feelings. That's why I try to listen to others carefully and respect their opinions. I'm sure this will be very helpful working in a team in-flight.

📑 5. 마음이 열려있는 사람

I think I am a quite open-minded person because I always love to socialize with people from various backgrounds and I always try to develop good relationships with the people I meet.

| 나의 답변 |

2. What are your strong points?

📑 1. My strong point is that I am not easily tired and do not get stressed because I have a healthy body and mind. Thus, I can fulfill the task at hand under any situation and I am still energetic even after hard work.

2. My strength is that I can handle emergencies very calmly and quickly. This is because I have the guts to handle any situation without panicking, and I can also act on my feet to take care of spontaneous situations.

-----

3. What are your weak points?

1. I am afraid I am not good at reading a map. So, I got lost a few times when I traveled to Europe last year. But whenever I had to ask for directions, I took it as a chance to talk to the locals and was able to make a lot of friends there.

2. I am afraid to say that I tend to be hasty. To overcome this, I am currently working towards taking things slower and thinking about the outcomes before starting my job.

4. How would your friends describe your personality?

1. Most of my friends told me that I am very friendly, outgoing, and a sociable person. Also they say I'm very fun to be with and easy to talk to. So, they always discuss their problems with me and like to listen to my opinions and take my advice.

5. Do you prefer to work alone or as a member of a team?

1. I prefer to work as a member of a team because I

have realized that in order to meet the team's goals, one must work together and not alone. When I was a student, I enjoyed working alone because my grades heavily depended on how much work I myself put into it. However, as I have learned, a flight attendant's job has a lot of time restrictions. So, I not only have to work efficiently by myself, but I also have to have good teamwork to reach our goals.

2. I think I am a great team player and prefer to work as a team because of my experiences working together in my school activities and in part-time jobs. Whenever we worked together, we finished our job much more easily and we also learned from each other. Through that, I've become more positive and an open-minded person.

| 나의 답변 |

면접관의 질문 의도를 파악하는 것이 성공적인 면접의 중요한 요소라고 할 수 있다. 개인의 성향과 적성을 알아볼 수 있는 최적의 질문 중의 하나가 취미이다. 따라서 취미는 승무원 직에 맞는 적성을 갖고 있음을 어필하기 위해 활동적이고 여러 사람들과 함께 할 수 있는 운동 등을 준비하는 것이 바람직하다.

질문 유형

1. What are your hobbies?/ What do you do in your spare time?/ How do you usually spend your free time?

1. I love to go hiking with my family or friends on weekends. Dobong Mountain is my favorite mountain of all time. It's very close to my house, so it's easy to go to and helps to keep me in good shape all year round.

2. I like getting up early and going for walks because I love the crisp morning air which makes me feel refreshed. Also, I go swimming at least twice a week.

I can swim 500m without stopping and swimming helps me be energetic all the time.

3. I really like all kinds of outdoor activities. Whenever I have free time, I like to bicycle along the Han River for at least 2 hours, enjoying the beautiful scenery. It gets me excited and full of energy. Through these things, I always feel fully recharged to carry out my daily life with vigor.

4. I like all kinds of ball games including tennis, badminton and squash. Whenever I'm free, I spend time with my family and friends playing those games. I think it's very fun and it's good for keeping you fit. (keeping you fit은 미국에서 자주 사람들이 쓰는 expression 상대방이 아니라 그냥 general 한 거)

5. I enjoy shopping with my friends. I usually go to Namdaemun Market, which is famous for affordable and trendy. I often just go to look around and have fun window-shopping.

6. Whenever I have free time, I like playing the piano or the violin. While playing masterpieces, I can release my stress and feel a sense of accomplishment. So, I meet with my orchestra and perform music

together once a month and I take time to learn how to harmonize with others as well.

7. I love cooking. Every Sunday I cook for my family because we are all busy during the weekdays so, the weekend is the only time I can treat them with my food. Also I often invite my friends and share my homemade food with them. I am so happy when people enjoy my food and get closer talking together while eating.

8. I try to read many different kinds of books. I especially like to read essays that stir me up with their practical and self-developed messages. Plus, through the books, I can experience other cultures and thoughts, which will help me with my future career.

| 나의 답변 |

Health Care

아무리 원해도 건강하지 않으면 할 수 없는 일이 승무원 일이다. 면접관은 이목구비가 예쁜 얼굴보다 건강한 생기가 넘치는 사람에게 더 호감을 느낀다. 나름대로 건강한 체력관리를 하고 있다는 것을 생기 있게 말하도록 한다.

* 질문의 예

1. Do you think you are healthy?

Yes, I think I am in good shape.

Yes, I consider myself to be fit.

Yes, I think I am healthy both physically and mentally.

2. How do you keep your health in check?/ What do you do
to keep up your health?

1. I try to exercise on a regular basis. I try to go to the gym at least three times a week. I am sure that this keeps me healthy physically and mentally.

2. I've been jogging every morning to keep myself fit for about 3 years. Through this, I believe I can start the day afresh. And also, I go swimming three times a week to keep myself energized. That's why I never catch a cold even during the wintertime.

3. I think it is important to have a variety of foods as much as possible to get all the necessary nutrients. And also, I take food supplements and vitamins to make up for any shortage of nutrients. I have always believed that healthy eating habits are very important in order to have a healthier body and mind.

4. I always take things positively and try not to get stressed in any situation. But if I do get stressed, I refresh my mind and body with a hot bath. I think a sound mind leads to a sound body so I always try to promote mental as well as physical fitness.

School Life

Why) 면접관들은 졸업예정자나 졸업한 지 1년 미만의 학생들이 일을 수행할 수 있는 역량과 자질이 있는지, 이 주제를 통하여 파악하고자 한다. 따라서 후보자들은 대학 캠퍼스, 동아리 활동, 봉사활동의 경험을 적극적으로 어필하여 타인을 배려하고 의존적이지 않은 성숙한 인성이 있다는 것을 증명하도록 노력하여야 한다. 본인에게 interpersonal skill, teamwork가 있다는 것을 보여주어야 하며, 승객을 상대할 수 있는 충분한 역량이 있음을 어필하여야 한다.

질문 유형

1. How was your (university/college/school) life?

1. I can say that I spent my school days very well. I always tried to exercise before going to school to keep myself in good shape and also prepared for my classes. After class, I studied for one or two hours in the library and then went to an English academy to develop my language skills. After finishing

everything, I relaxed at home and took some time to reflect on the day. This was my daily school life.

2. I consider myself to have been a diligent student. I never missed classes and I participated actively in all my classes. Because of this, I received high grades and during this time I was also involved in a lot of extra curricular activities. Through these things, I obtained greater interpersonal and social skills as well.

2. What is your major?/ Tell me about your major.

1. My major was German Language and Literature. Through my major, I learned how to read and speak in German and had chances to get to know the culture. I especially, loved to read German novels

such as Hermann Hesse, one of Germany's leading Novelist. If I am hired as a flight attendant for your airline, I can, not only make German announcements but also help German passengers while speaking their native language.

2. I majored in Aviation Tourism Management. Through my major, I learned practical skills and knowledge necessary to become a flight attendant, such as Food and Beverage Service, in-flight English etc. Because of this, I am quite confident that I'm ready to be a member of a professional cabin crew.

3. Why did you choose your major?/ What made you choose your major?

1. Since I was very young, I have been interested in

other languages and cultures. I especially wanted to know about European Culture, so I chose my major to satisfy my interests. As a potential global flight attendant, I believe it was the best major for me.

2. Being a flight attendant has been a lifelong dream of mine. I chose my major because I believed that this program offered me the best courses and professors to prepare in becoming a flight attendant. I am sure I made the right choice and that this will be the cornerstone for my success.

| 나의 답변 |

4. What kind of activities did you do in your college life?/ What were your extra curricular activities during school?

1. I was the student representative in my major department for 2 years. Through this experience, I

learned lots of things such as interpersonal—skills, listening skills, and responsibility. Most of all, I realized how important it was to cooperate with one another to accomplish the shared goals.

📧 2. I was a member of a volunteer group. We often visited welfare centers to teach English for underprivileged children and played with them. We tried to give them better educational opportunities and when their academic abilities improved, I was overjoyed.

| 나의 답변 |

5. What was the most memorable moment in your college life? Tell me about your most impressive college experience.

📧 1. When I was a sophomore, I went to Australia to take an English course during my summer vacation. At that time, I made a lot of foreign friends from all over the world and I learned how to mingle and communicate with them. It was a very wonderful experience.

2. Every summer vacation, I went to a rural area in Korea to help the farmers with the hard work. Doing farming on a hot day was not easy but when they gave us a lot of thanks, I felt greatly rewarded. Thus, I learned how to understand a person in another job. It was a very meaningful experience.

| 나의 답변 |

8 Work Experience

서비스 관련 경력, 간호원 경력에 항공사는 매우 큰 관심을 보인다. 그러나 승무원과 관련 경력이 아니어도 그곳에서 배운 경력이 앞으로 승무원의 일에 어떤 긍정적인 영향을 주는지를 피력해야 한다(ex. 팀워크 등). 꼬리에 꼬리를 무는 질문으로 발전할 경우가 매우 높다. 직장을 그만둔 이유나 어려웠던 점등에 대해서는 지나치게 솔직하게 부정적인 경우를 말하지 말고 해결하기 위해 노력했던 사례를 중심으로 이야기해야 한다.

질문 유형

1. Can you tell me about your work/ part-time job experience?

📧 1. Certainly. I have had experiences with part-time jobs such as serving meals in a restaurant and as a barista in a coffee shop for about 2 years. They were very precious experiences for learning the service mind and communication skills as a service provider. Through that experience, I found that my aptitude for service was very suitable to be a flight attendant.

2. Certainly. I was a staff in the theater as a part-time job during my college years. I welcomed guests at the entrance and ushered them to their seat. Through that experience, I learned how to talk to customers in a polite manner with a correct attitude. And I found that maintaining good relations with other colleagues is also very important for dealing with hectic situations.

3. I received an opportunity to get a job at a hotel for one year. I worked at different departments such as the front desk, concierge, and room service. My responsibilities included hotel reservations, guest contact at a concierge, and maintaining facilities. Through these experiences, I learned how to interact with customers and manage challenging interactions.

4. I worked as a secretary at ONAIR Company for 3 years. My main duties were managing the schedule of my boss, arranging meetings, escorting guests, and receiving phone calls for my boss. At first, I

went through some difficulties when I had to handle so many things all at once. But as time went on, I learned how to prioritize, and multi-task and so, could skillfully handle the different assignments. Thanks to my job experience, I am now confident when dealing with many tasks.

5. I've been working with ONAIR Company for 2 years at the overseas marketing department. I had a lot of chances to work with foreigners, and I learned how to communicate with them efficiently. And when they visited Korea, I was the one who showed them the attractions in Seoul, which I love to do in order to share our wonderful culture.

2. What do you do for living?/ What do you do at the moment?

1. At the moment, I'm still a student at AIR University. However, I do work on a part-time basis on weekends as a barista at a coffee shop.

2. Currently, I don't have a job because I just graduated from my university and I'm now spending time to concentrate on becoming a flight attendant in your company.

3. Right now, I am teaching English to young children at an English language institute.
To be honest, it's not easy handling young kids all day long, but through this experience, I have learned how to be patient while handling young kids and know that it will be very helpful for working as a flight attendant in your company.

| 나의 답변 |

3. What did you learn through your part time jobs?

1. Thankfully, I have learned how to serve different types of customers and deal with unexpected situations at the coffee shop because I had many customers and I had to meet their needs individually day by day. It was a very challenging experience for me and I'm sure that I am well prepared to deal with unexpected passengers on board.

2. I learned so many things through my job. First of all, I learned how important teamwork is for accomplishing team goals. I tried to maintain good relationships with my colleagues all the time and it helped me in dealing with a lot of duties.

3. When I had an internship in Australia, I worked with a lot of colleagues from various countries. It was a very exciting experience for me to be able to learn different cultures and hear diverse thoughts. I especially learned how to come to an agreement with different opinions. We respected everyone's opinions and enjoyed discussing them.

Through this, I became a person who could understand and respect other people's way of thinking

 온에어 인터뷰

and their culture.

---

4. Why do you want to leave your job?

🗩 1. When I worked at a hotel, I really enjoyed my job because I could interact with a variety of customers. I was especially overjoyed when a customer gave me compliments for my service. But I sincerely look forward to accomplishing my dream, which is to work as a flight attendant. So, I decided to leave my job to have more time to prepare for this interview.

🗩 2. To be honest, I enjoyed my office job but I always wanted to work more actively and dynamically, visiting different countries and meeting many people.

I am sure a flight attendant job is the right one for me and even just thinking about it gets me excited. I believe I am ready for a new career.

 온에어 인터뷰

9 Overseas Experience

해외경험에 관한 질문은 승무원 직에 적성이 맞는지를 평가하는 중요한 질문이다. 세계관, 즉 다른 나라 문화에 대한 관심도와 다른 문화에 잘 융화할 수 있는지를 알아보는 것으로, 외국 경험이 없다 해도 이것이 탈락의 원인이 되지는 않으므로 다른 방법으로 외국 문화에 관심을 갖고 있다는 것을 어필하도록 한다.

1. Have you ever been overseas?/ Have you ever been abroad?

1. When I was a junior in college, I went backpacking in Europe during my summer vacation. While there, I spent every moment excited and wide-eyed, visiting over 10 countries in only a month. For a long time, I had been eager to visit the famous attractions and museums to see the timeless masterpieces. It was a great experience that I will never forget.

2. When I was a sophomore in college, I went to Sydney,

Australia to attend an English training course for 6 months. While I was studying, I experienced working in a seafood restaurant in Darling Harbor on a part time basis. It was an amazing opportunity to serve foreign customers and gain an understanding for their culture.

3. Yes, I lived in America as an exchanging student for a year. I studied at a University located quite far away from any big cities in order to avoid meeting Korean students. I wanted to be able to practice speaking in English with local students and become fluent quickly. It was a very valuable and memorable time for improving my language skills and learning about American culture while mingling with the students.

4. Well I haven't traveled to another country yet. But because of this, I have tried to gain a wider knowledge and perspective of the world through Internet surfing and foreign TV shows. And I continued to make efforts to gain more information. I am sure this will help me to be able to answer many questions in-flight if a passenger asks about information on travel attractions around the world.

5. Unfortunately, I haven't visited any countries yet but I have traveled to a lot of places in Korea. Whenever I have free time, I always make a plan to go somewhere in Korea. I especially nowadays have become interested in visiting places that have been filmed in Korean TV shows. It's very fun and interesting. But in the near future I hope I can visit Hong Kong as a flight attendant in your airline.

| 나의 답변 |

---

2. What is the difference between Koreans and Europeans?/ How different are they from Koreans?

1. The biggest difference between Europeans and Koreans is that Europeans are quite simply dressed

for their daily life activities. They don't mind wearing
the same dress every day as long as it is neat and
tidy. Also I was a bit surprised that they spend
hot summer days without air conditioning systems
and they don't seem to even mind sweating a lot. I
was very impressed by their practicality and frugal
lifestyle and I learned how to save and use materials
in a constructive way.

3. Have you ever been in difficult situations while traveling in
another country?

1. Well, to be honest, I never had any difficulties. I
really had great times enjoying the food and learning

about the culture, and even making a lot of friends from all over the world. I still keep in touch with them. They were really wonderful experiences.

2. While travelling in the countryside of France, I had some difficulties communicating in English. Especially when ordering food in a restaurant, they sometimes couldn't understand what I was saying. But it didn't take much time before we understood each other through using non-verbal communication skills like gestures, and later on, they anticipated my needs and were very caring. I was very impressed by their sincere service.

| 나의 답변 |

4. If you became a flight attendant, where would you like to go first? And why?

📑 1. I'd like to go New York first. I would like to see my classmates from my University and the owner of the home—stay house which I stayed in(가정민박 주인). Since I have left New York, I miss them a lot and I'm looking forward to seeing them again. They will be delighted to see me in your airline's uniform.

📑 2. I'd like to visit Paris first because Paris, in my opinion, is the most attractive place in the world. I want to visit all the museums, especially the Louvre, to see the masterpieces as well as the Eiffel Tower, for it is the landmark of Paris. Also I am eager to visit the Palace of Versailles to experience the royal family's lifestyle. Even just thinking about it gets me very excited.

| 나의 답변 |

 온에어 인터뷰

5. If you can recommend a place to visit in Korea, where would you like to recommend?

1. If foreigners are visit Korea for the first time, then I would definitely recommend Myung Dong first. It is the center of Seoul and there are a lot of shopping areas. People can also enjoy several kinds of different Korean food and international food as well. Whenever I go there, I feel so connected, seeing many fashionable people in the streets and sometimes I also see street performances. Also I can buy high quality accessories or clothes at a good price in the street stands. This is another great benefit from visiting Myung Dong.

| 나의 답변 |

10 Self Introduction

* Self Introduction 작성 순서

자기소개는 특정한 형식은 없으나 일반적인 생각의 흐름을 따라가는 것이 좋다. 즉 누군가를 처음 만났을 때 그 사람에 대해 알고 싶은 점을 떠올리면 자기소개 순서에 대해 쉽게 이해 하게 된다.

1. 학생으로 직장 경험이 많지 않은 지원자

   1) 도입인사

   2) 이름

   3) 학교, 전공

   4) 특별활동, 봉사활동

   5) 지원 동기, 포부

(SAMPLE ANSWER)

1. Good morning. It's very nice meeting you today. My name is Eun Hae Kim but you can call me Grace. I'm 21 years old and I'm a senior majoring in education

at 00 University. I consider myself to be an active student because I have been involved in many school activities such as being a member of the English debate club, where we talk to each other only in English. That's why I am so confident in my English speaking skills and it also helped me build many relationships with people during school. Also I was involved in a volunteer organization in order to help those in need in our society. Through this, I found out that I feel great joy when I share something with others. Besides the many activities I was a part of, my good grades in class proved that I was a diligent student. So I'm sure that if you give me a chance I can show you that I am an outstanding cabin crewmember who can be faithful to my seniors and trustworthy to my colleagues. I will do my best to enhance the reputation of your company's airline.

2. 관련 학과 전공자

1) 도입인사

2) 이름 소개

3) 학교, 전공

4) 서비스업종에서 아르바이트

5) 외국어 능력, 해외경험

6) 지원 동기, 포부

2. Hello, everyone. I'm honored to see you here today. My name is Eun Hae Kim and I graduated from 00 College last February. My major was Aviation Management and I chose my major to prepare myself to become a flight attendant. In my major, I learned a lot of useful skills about food & beverage service, and in-flight communication skills. Also I have had job experiences in customer service, such as an internship at the Hyatt hotel for 3 months. Through these experiences I have put these skills to practice so I could learn how to anticipate customer's needs and be proactive. Plus, staying in the Philippines for 6 months was a very memorable experience for me in order to understand the different cultures. I can never forget the precious memory of mingling with many other people from various countries. That's why, your

professional, multilingual cabin crew from diverse ethnicities is one of my main reasons for applying to your airline. Based on what I've experienced, I will do my best as a flight attendant to represent your company as the best airline in the world.

3. 장기 해외경험이 있는 지원자

  1) 도입인사
  2) 이름 소개
  3) 학교, 전공
  4) 외국어 능력, 해외경험
  5) 경력
  6) 지원 동기, 포부

(SAMPLE ANSWER)

3. Good morning. It's a great pleasure to be able to introduce myself to you. My name is Eun Hae Kim but you can call me Faith. I just graduated from 00 University with an honors degree in English language and literature. It's been a dream to become a flight attendant since I was very young. In order to

become a person that suits the global airlines, I have developed my English and Chinese communication skills and have tried to learn global mannerisms to understand diverse cultures. When I went to America as an exchanging student for two years, I attended not only language schools but also joined international aid agencies that care for refugees. It was very precious experience to be mature enough to understand other's situations and how to care for people who need help. Also, I have had several part time job experiences in service fields, through which I developed a service-minded attitude and interpersonal skills. Therefore, I believe that I am well qualified to become a good flight attendant and I am ready to devote all my passion and efforts as a travelling partner for your passengers.

4. 일반사무직종의 직장 유경험의 지원자

  1) 도입인사

  2) 이름

  3) 학교, 전공

4) 경력

5) 지원 동기, 포부

4. Good afternoon, everyone. First of all, thank you for giving me this chance today. My name is Eun Hae Kim but you can call me Lucy. I graduated from 00 University in Business administration. Currently, I've been working at 00 company for more than 2 years and I am in the overseas marketing department. I think positive energy represents who I am. I always try to see the bright side of things and work to achieve my goals under any situation. Indeed I am always willing to learn new things everyday and it makes me challenge myself towards a new career without any hesitations. I sometimes have to pick clients up at the airport from other countries and arrange hotels for them. At first, I felt embarrassed when I was not able to catch their preferences since I wanted to treat them as best as possible. But soon, I found out it was quite easy to please them because of my considerate personality, which helped me to

understand their culture and differences. Now, I really enjoy working with people from other countries and sharing different thoughts and experiences. Through my job, I believe I became a person who can accept multicultural diversity. So, if you give me a chance to take the first step toward my new career, I will do my best to have confidence in satisfying your international passengers.

Job of a Flight Attendant

미소와 친절, 매너를 갖춘 최고의 서비스 전문직이며, 소속 항공사의 이미지인 객실승무원은 승객의 안전을 책임지고 승객이 목적지까지 편안하게 도착할 수 있도록 보살피는 역할을 한다. 또한, 기내 시설물, 엔터테인먼트, 식·음료 등의 서비스를 승객에게 제공하는 중요한 인적자원으로서 단정한 용모, 미소와 예절, 항공업무지식과 글로벌 직업인으로서의 언어소통능력 등 다양한 자질들이 요구되어진다. 또한, 기내라는 특수하고도 제한적인 근무환경으로 인해 예상치 못하게 발생하는 비상상황에 대응할 수 있는 순발력 있는 대처능력도 필요하다.

1. What is the job description of a F/A?

1. I think that the job description of a F/A is to provide a safe, comfortable and enjoyable flight for all the passengers. I know that there are many duties in this job, but I believe safety has to be the first priority of the job.

2. I would like to say that a F/A is the service provider as well as the lifeguard in-flight. They do all kinds of duties such as delivering beverages, meal services, and maintaining a good environment in the cabin, etc. Also, part of the outstanding professionalism of this job involves carrying first aid to a sick passenger and rescuing their life.

| 나의 답변 |

2. Why do crewmembers have to look good for the customers?

1. I think a service provider has a responsibility to look good, not only for him/herself, but also for the customers. Because by looking presentable, they can not only respect themselves but also communicate to

others that they respect and care for their customers.
Also, the company has benefits from F/As looking
good because they help create a positive image of the
airline.

2. I believe F/As have to look good for their
passengers because the passengers appreciate such
professionalism and therefore will treat them like
one. Also I think F/As feel good about themselves
and their job and therefore gain more confidence
when interacting with their passengers while looking
respectable. I think this is a positive circle that
is initiated by an effort to look good and I believe
looking good must involve both physical appearance
and behavior.

| 나의 답변 |

3. What are the duties of a F/A?/ Can you tell me the duties
of a F/A in which they should be carried out? (Stages of a
flight can be viewed as having four main stages in which
they should be carried out.)

Tip. 단계별로 답변을 정리해 본다.

Stage 1) Pre take-off prior to passenger boarding (이륙 전
승객탑승이 시작되기 전 단계)

1. I think a F/A starts their duties from the moment
they board. Because safety and service should
be their focus, I think they need to check the
emergency equipment and security checks prior to
passenger boarding and they also have to prepare
the service preparation as much as possible for the
efficiencies.

2. I believe safety is the most important duty of this
job. Prior to passenger boarding, I think they need to
report any missing items or unserviceable emergency
equipment so that remedial action can be taken before
the flight departs. Also F/As have to check to ensure
no suspicious items or unauthorized personnel are on
board at security checks.

3. I think F/As need to be responsible for dressing the cabin and ensuring the cleanliness of the seats, seat pockets, tables and headrest covers etc. Also, they should dress toilets and prepare amenities such as hand towels, headsets and overnight kits etc. before passenger boarding.

What does the term 'amenities' mean?

'Amenities' refer to items/facilities e.g hand towels, headsets, magazines, blankets, postcards, playing cards etc. that are provided on board for passengers use.

| 나의 답변 |

1. I think, for a F/A, making a good first impression on their passengers is very important. And this depends on how they interact with their passengers. So, during passenger boarding, they should greet them warmly with a sincere smile and direct them to their allocated seats. And also, on this stage, a F/A should respond accordingly when a passenger asks to hang their coats/jackets/suit bags.

2. I think one of the important duties of a F/A is the safety demo before take-off to guide passengers in evacuation in case of emergency situations. After that, they have to carry out pre take-off checks for safety such as seeing if the passenger's seat belt is fastened, tables are latched, if the seat-backs are upright and aisles are cleared etc.

3. I think making in-flight announcements is one of their main duties. I believe the in-flight announcement is very important for the service and safety of the passengers. If the aircraft passes through turbulence, they need to make an

announcement for the passengers and also they should inform them of service-related things through it. I believe in-flight announcements provide another way of service by means of voice.

Stage 3) After take-off(이륙 후)

1. A F/A offers amenities, menu cards and conduct beverages or meal services to passengers to enjoy the flight after take-off. Also they distribute passenger documents such as C.I.Q. forms and sometimes they help to complete the immigration forms for passengers if they ask. They also sell in-flight duty free items.

C.I.Q.(customs, immigration, quarantine)

2. For the hygiene of the cabin, I think F/As have a responsibility to ensure toilet cleanliness. I think it is necessary to especially increase the frequency of checking the toilets, such as when the loading is full or after waking the passengers up in the morning. I am sure, no matter how excellent the service was, if toilet hygiene was not good enough, passengers will not be satisfied with the flight.

3. I think one of the duties of F/As is to maintain the tidiness of the cabin e.g collecting used items and also attending to individual's needs, particularly children/infants, physically challenged passengers etc. Also, F/As have to spend time with passengers. And to achieve this they need to be visible to their passengers, especially trying to have small talk with the bored passengers. I am sure this will make their service special and memorable.

4. I believe the most important duty of a F/A is the handling of safety. They need to conduct drills in case of emergency—situations and apply first aid if passengers are sick. I am sure this makes the job of a F/A more professional and that it demands higher

qualifications than for other service industries.

Stage 4) After landing(착륙 후)

1. I think safety always comes first in this job. I am sure that not only the handling of the unexpected emergency situations but also that routine safety is very important.

Whenever I flew abroad, I found out that passengers frequently stood up while the aircraft was taxing after landing. I think this is very dangerous so F/As need to ensure passengers to remain seated and overhead lockers remain closed until the aircraft completely stops and the seat belt sign is off. Also, after landing, a F/A should ensure that all the passengers have disembarked and check any left items for passengers.

(Advantages/Likes)

1. There are a lot of advantages of becoming a F/A such as the opportunity to travel around the world, meet a lot of new people, and experience many different cultures. I am sure this will extend my views, perspectives, and thoughts of this world.

2. I believe working as a F/A will bring me many opportunities to meet people and work with various crewmembers from other countries. This will help me to develop my English language skills and interpersonal skills as well. I am also very excited to learn about various cultures while traveling to other countries.

3. I know this job has a lot of good points. Above all I like this job due to the dynamic schedule since the work involves traveling around the world. Also a F/A job has a lot of days off compared to other jobs, so I can spend my spare time developing good skills,

which will improve the quality of my life.

(Disadvantages/Dislikes)

1. I know a F/A job has a few disadvantages, such as experiencing jetlag, working long hours and an irregular schedule time. Also sometimes, they have to deal with difficult passengers that can emotionally affect a F/A. However, I see more of the positive side of a F/A job and I am also exercising regularly to improve body strength. And concerning difficult passengers, I will try not to take it personally and be unemotional to control myself. Furthermore, I like to manage such challenging interactions and solve problems.

2. Well, I know this job isn't perfect, as all jobs aren't. Most of all, I will not able to attend family events and spend time with my family or friends on holidays because of the irregular working hours. But nowadays, I can access the Internet anywhere and make video calls to them from all over the world and show them pictures of other countries. So, even though we are far apart, I can still feel like I'm back home and can constantly check up on them.

3. Unlike most office jobs in which the working hours are regular, this job as a cabin attendant requires me to follow a highly irregular work pattern. The time I spend on and off duty may cover any hour of the day or any day of the month, depending on the work schedule, which is given to me every month. I think it demands a highly strong body condition to overcome the unstable life cycle but on the bright side, I will not feel bored by a daily-routine life.

온에어 인터뷰

SEQ 12 Reason for application

1. Why do you want to be a Flight Attendant?

1. When I flew to Hawaii during a family vacation trip, I was very impressed with the service the flight attendants gave. They kept people comfortable and pleased during the flight and even though the flying time was more than 12 hours, they never stopped smiling and had good manners until the end of the flight. Also, they treated all the passengers equally, regardless of their nationalities, conversing in fluent English. They looked even more professional and gorgeous in their uniforms that were perfectly groomed. Since then, I have decided to become a flight attendant hoping that my life can be full of opportunities for professional career developments.

2. The most attractive reason for being a flight attendant is that I will be able to work with multi lingual people from all over the world. When I was on board your airline last year, it was very impressive to

see cabin crewmembers that mixed well with different backgrounds and nationalities. Seeing them enjoy their working environment while supporting each other was enough to gain my interest. I am sure my people skills and outgoing personality will glow in this working environment and I will adapt very easily while enjoying myself.

3. Since I was young, I had a strong curiosity about other parts of the world. So, I have always wanted to visit as many various places as possible and experience their culture in the world. Even just thinking about it gets me, very excited. That's why it has been a dream of mine to become a flight attendant and also why I am looking forward to meeting many people from all over the word while working at the same time. I am sure that I will broaden my view further, sharing my thoughts with foreign people and also learning from them. I believe this is the right job I want to be in and I will do my best to contribute successfully for continuous growth in my global perspective.

4. I want to be a flight attendant because this is the

job I enjoy working in. And also, I always have been deeply thinking about my career and my future for a long time. So now, I am sure that this is the job that offers me the most rewarding benefits. Because through many part time jobs and volunteer experiences, I learned how great it is to be able to help someone. I always kept in mind the old saying to 'Treat others the way you want to be treated. I will try my best to serve from my heart and sincerely help your passengers as a cabin crewmember of your airline.

2. What made you apply to our company?/ Why do you want to work for this airline?

1. (Cathay Pacific Airways) I know that there are a lot of good airlines in the world. But Cathay Pacific Airways is the most admirable company for me, which is why I always have wanted to join. As I have learned, your company recruits flight attendants from 11 Asian countries, and I think this makes your company differentiable among other airlines. Most of all, you are famous for having perfect safety procedures, as well as having excellent in-flight service. Also, you have never had any issued accidents or mistakes. Your continuous efforts to contribute to help the underprivileged children, such as Unicef, also made me more determined to apply for your company. I really want to contribute to my future job as a flight attendant at Cathay Pacific Airways and I believe that I would spend amazing days while working with my colleagues.

2. (Emirates Airline)First of all, your airline that is growing and expanding rapidly worldwide with no airline comparing to it, and your professional,

multilingual cabin crews from more than 120 countries are two of the main reasons for applying to your company. I'd be very excited to work with crewmembers from different countries and we could learn from each other. I would like to show my ability in a big company like yours and expand my career, for I want to be a successful partner with you, and not just a service provider. I will do my best to be a contributing employee for your company.

3. (LCC– Low Cost Carrier) The reason why I applied to your airline is that your company is growing very quickly with an excellent reputation. I would like to contribute to your growth successfully by presenting my abilities to you. I am sure you will be one of the major leading airlines in the near future and I would be very proud of myself to be one of the talented cabin crewmembers of your airline.

13 Qualification

1. Why should we hire you?

📑 1. I see that there are a lot of applicants here, but I believe I am the right person for your company. My overseas experience shows you that I am great at speaking English and that I'm enough of an open-minded person to relate to various passengers. I have also always been able to achieve my goals under any situation and my best qualities actually come out when there is a crisis. I'm quite steady as well as strong, so I am able to handle things very calmly during emergencies. Most of all, I am willing to go the extra mile and take the initiative to ensure the well-being and comfort of your passengers.

📑 2. I think you should hire me because I believe I am the right person for this company. I consider myself to be well qualified as a flight attendant because through my job experiences, I gained great interpersonal skills and a service-oriented mind. Besides, I am a great team player and able to synchronize with all kinds of people. I will do all that I can to make your passengers feel like they have chosen the right airline to fly with. I am sure that I will be a valuable asset to your company.

3. I am the right person for your company because I believe that my various experiences in the service industry and especially my 3 years of customer service experience at Hyatt hotel will be an important asset for your airline. Through that time, I gained a wide knowledge of service skills and learned how to handle customer's needs effectively. I am sure I am well prepared now and will do my best to be a valuable cabin crewmember at your company.

| 나의 답변 |

1. I am very confident of my qualifications to be a flight attendant because I know I am better prepared than other people. Because ever since high school this has been my dream, I decided on the corresponding major in college to learn more about aviation. Plus, I learned the correct attitude of a service provider. I'm also confident in speaking in English, especially because an in-flight English course was one of my favorite subjects in college. I am eager to work as a flight attendant, using the knowledge and skills that I've obtained during school.

2. I know that this job requires a lot of body strength in order to endure irregular schedules and time differences. I am not only confident of my fit physical state but also of my trained mental state. I don't get stressed easily and am enough of an easy going person to make people feel comfortable to be around me. I believe I easily adapt and adjust myself to any new environment, which is an important qualification as a flight attendant. Now, I

am ready to devote myself to this job and I am sure

I will become better suited for this job through your

training course.

Visions and Aspiration

1. What is your vision for your life?

1. I see my future as a professional flight attendant of your airline. I'd like to work as long as possible, contributing to your growth by developing myself through continual training. Also I will keep learning other languages such as Japanese, Chinese and French. I want to talk with my passengers from these countries in their language without any difficulties and they will surely feel more at ease in-flight. I am sure I can achieve all of these things and hope to succeed in my career at your company.

2. I definitely would like to be a flight attendant of your company, traveling around the world, meeting many people and developing my language skills. As I have noticed, your company keeps expanding worldwide and I'd like to have this great opportunity to keep enhancing my career for as long as possible.

2. Where do you want to be in your life in 10 years?

1. In ten years I would like to describe myself as a premier flight attendant of your company. As a role model for my junior crewmembers, I will try my best to perform as best as I can by contributing good team work and service skills. If it's possible, I also want to be a training instructor to train my junior crewmembers through the knowledge I have gained

during my experiences. Thus, I am looking forward to receiving the chance to show you my abilities.

---

3. What is your biggest accomplishment in your life?

1. Well, there have been many things in my life that I achieved so far, like entering my University and receiving a scholarship from my major. But honestly, receiving this interview opportunity is my biggest accomplishment. So, I am eager to be a member of your airline.

In-flight situation- Service

(Service 란?)

1. What is the definition of service?/ How would you define customer service?

1. I think the definition of service is providing various elements such as food, beverages, and other amenities to satisfy customer's needs. But I believe what makes the service special and memorable is the friendliness and genuine concern that a service provider shows to their customers. So I believe that it's always better to be proactive and anticipate the customer's needs to show consideration towards the customer.

2. I think service is the act of making the customer happy when they are treated by a service provider. One can make the customer happy through various elements but I want to define good service as the ability to put oneself into the customer's shoes to understand the customer's situation, feelings and motives as well. This is why I always believe the best service comes straight from the heart and that the

customers should be able to feel the sincere actions.

(Anticipating- 승객의 필요를 미리 볼 수 있는 서비스자질)

1. If a passenger looks bored how would you help him/her?

1. First of all, I would approach the passenger and recommend the passenger in-flight entertainment programs such as watching a movie, listening to music, or reading materials. If the passenger accepts,

I would kindly give him/her further instructions about our programs in detail and also bring him/her some snacks with beverages to enjoy their time.

2. Well, I would try to have small talk with the passenger after judging whether the passenger would like to be talked to or not. While making small talk, I would try to create a warm atmosphere and also try to find out if the needs of the passenger are being met.

2. If a passenger is having trouble sleeping how can you help him/her?

📧 1. I'll offer the passenger a hot drink such as chamomile tea, which is helpful for sleeping. But if he still cannot sleep, I would suggest to him in-flight entertainment programs until he feels like sleeping.

| 나의 답변 |

---

3. If a passenger is cold what would you do?

📧 1. Of course, I would offer an extra blanket. But if there are no extra ones, I would check whether the other passengers feel cold or not. If they are cold, I would ask my section leader to adjust the cabin temperature and I would make sure that all the passengers feel comfortable. After that, of course, I would offer a cup of hot tea.

---

4. During meal service, if a passenger is working, what would you do?

1. First of all, I would ask the passenger whether he/she wants to take his/her meal now or after finishing their work. If he/she wants to eat now then I would help him/her in clearing up the table, which is used as the meal tray, by offering a bag to keep the objects that he/she is not using off the table. But if he/she wants to eat after their work is done, I would ask him/her about their choice of meal to make a note and make sure to come back to him/her later.

5. During passenger boarding, if you see a mother with her infant, what would you do?

1. At first, I would greet and assist the mother with her belongings, guiding them to their seat, and then I would help her and her baby settle down comfortably in her seat. After that, I would offer an infant seat belt and brief her on how to use it for the safety of her baby and a plastic bag to throw away trash like used diapers during the flight. I am sure it will help the mother in keeping their seat clean until arrival. And finally, I would tell the mother that I will install a baby bassinet for her baby after take-off. Before I

leave, I would encourage her to call me at any time for assistance and assure her of my willingness to help.

6. How would you help UM(unaccompanied minor) passengers during boarding?

1. I think children who are not accompanied by their parents probably need additional care and assistance. I would assist them with their baggage and take them

to their seat.

And I would introduce myself and let them know that I am there for them. Also I would teach them how to use the call button, fasten/unfasten the seat belt and brief them on the locations of the toilets. Finally, I would assure them that I am always pleased to help them and would encourage them to use the call button should they need any assistance.

7. How would you handle the Plump passengers? (Bigger than ordinary passenger's e.g. obese passengers,

🗨 1. I think that they may need an extension seat belt for take-off and landing. When offering them the extension seat belts, I will talk tactfully so that they are not embarrassed.

| 나의 답변 |

----

8. How would you help the blind and deaf passengers?

🗨 1. I think establishing effective communication is very important. I would always address blind passengers by name and use more verbal communication. On the other hand, I would use more body language such as gestures when communicating with deaf passengers. And I would pay more attention to their needs without causing them any unnecessary embarrassment such as not offering reading materials to blind passengers or headsets to deaf passengers. Lastly, I would encourage them to use the call button should they need any assistance e.g. going to the bathroom.

 온에어 인터뷰

There are actually 4 steps we must follow

1st Apologize 사과한다. ex) I'm sorry/ I apologize.

2nd Explain 상황에 대한 이해를 시켜준다. ex) Unfortunately we've run out of beef.

3rd Express Empathy 공감을 표현해 마음을 연다. ex) I know that you really wanted some more.

4th Offer an alternative 대안을 제시한다. ex) May I offer you fish instead?

질문 유형

1. What would you say if a passenger wants to have the choice with beef that have all been taken?

1. First of all, I would apologize to the passenger and explain to him/her that we have limited choice of meals in-flight and all the choices with beef have been taken by other passengers. And then I would try to persuade the passenger to take the other choice, but if this is not what he/she wants, I would see if I could bring him/her anything else as alternatives and

inform my section leader of what happened for any
further action.

----

2. During the meal service, a passenger says that he
requested a vegetarian meal, which is not on board. What
would you do?

1. At first, I would ask the passenger if he requested
his special meal through our reservations office
and I would check his passenger information letter
with my section leader on whether he requested it
or not. And if he requested it, I would apologize to

him of the mistake on our part. Then I would try to be resourceful in satisfying the passenger with something else such as fruit, salad etc. And of course, if the passenger has to wait a while, I would offer him something to drink first while the meal is being prepared.

---

3. If a foreign object was found in a passenger's meal, what would you do?

1. I would apologize to the passenger for this mistake and

change his/her meal immediately. Also I would try to find anything else that I could get him/her to make up for this fault. Afterwards, I would report to my section leader about this incident and keep an eye on the passenger until the end of the flight to make sure that he/she can enjoy the rest of the flight.

4. What would you do, if you spilled a cup of hot coffee on a passenger due to sudden turbulence?

1. First of all, I would sincerely apologize to the passenger and check whether the passenger got burned or not. If the passenger is fine, I would offer a dry towel and help the passenger to clean up right

away and also if the seat is wet, I would offer another seat if possible. Then I would inform my section leader of this incident and offer a laundry service to the passenger that the passenger can use upon his/her arrival afterwards. And of course, I would pay extra attention to the passenger to make sure he/she enjoys the rest of the flight.

| 나의 답변 |

5. What would you say if a passenger asks you for a drink or cocktail which you have never heard of?

1. First I would apologize and tell them that we don't

carry the drink. And I would suggest an appropriate alternative. And for a cocktail, I would ask what the ingredients are to the passenger and if they are available, I would make it for passenger, but if they are not available, I would apologize and suggest an appropriate alternative to the passenger.

6. What would you say if a passenger asks for a business or first class beverage?

📑 1. I would apologize to the passenger and say that we don't have it in the economy class. And I would try to persuade the passenger to accept our alternatives but if he/she still insists to have the beverage, I would check with my section leader to see if it is possible.

Safety는 승객의 생명과도 직결되는 매우 중요한 사안으로써 service보다 우선시되어야 하는 문제이다. Safety에 대한 질문은 일회성으로 끝나는 경우보다 동일한 질문을 심문하듯이 파고드는 경우가 많은데, 이것은 면접자들이 안전에 대한 문제를 승객과 타협하지 않고 고수하는지를 보려고 하는 것이다. 이때는 동일한 답변을 앵무새처럼 반복 답하는 것보다 강한 의지를 보여주는 key expression을 먼저 말하고 답하는 것이 중요하다.

| Key expression |

ex) I believe safety is the number one priority.

I believe safety always has to come before other things.

I will not negotiate about matters related to safety with passengers.

I will not compromise on the problem of safety.

1. How would you handle a nervous flyer?

1. First of all I would approach the passenger and check the passenger's condition. And when I talk to the passenger I would be very careful not to ask directly if the passenger is nervous or if he/she is a nervous flyer. And to reassure and comfort the nervous passenger, I would explain that many people can feel this way while flying and that his/her feeling is not unusual. Then I would suggest the passenger some in-flight entertainment programs such as watching movies, listening to the radio, or reading materials to take his/her mind off of things. And I would offer him/her a blanket to curl up in and a cup of hot tea to relax. After all this, I would check on the passenger from time to time until the end of the flight.

| 나의 답변 |

2. What if a passenger smokes in the toilet, how would you handle the situation?

1. I would ask the passenger to put his cigarette out immediately, because smoking in-flight is strictly forbidden for safety. I would talk to him politely but firmly to make sure he never smokes again while flying. And I would also bring some snacks and beverages to help him to pass the time and not think of smoking. And I would definitely check the toilet thoroughly to see whether there are any fumes or a fire to prevent further fire hazards. Then I would report this to my section leader to be on alert for any other situations.

2ND same question

Well, unfortunately, he smokes again one hour later.

What would you do?

2. I believe safety has to be the number one priority. I would never compromise on matters related to safety. So I would talk to him more firmly than before to stop him from smoking in-flight, and I would explain and give a verbal warning to him that smoking in-flight is against the aviation regulations so if he smokes again I cannot help but take further action to stop this.

3. What would you do if a drunken passenger keeps asking
for more alcohol?

1. I know that being drunk in-flight is quite dangerous.
So I would ask the passenger to slow down on his
drinks for his safety and I would try to serve another
drink such as ice water or orange juice to relieve him/
her of a hangover. And I would inform my colleagues
about the drunken passenger in order to avoid serving
any more alcohol to him/her.

2ND same question

1. I believe safety must come before service all the time. Even though he/she insists on having more alcohol, I will not serve him/her more of it. If he/she is not compliant, I will report this to my section leader and take further action to avoid causing a greater problem in the future.

| 나의 답변 |

4. What would you do if a passenger wants to go to the toilet during turbulence?

📧 1. I would ask the passenger to sit down and fasten his/her seat belt immediately for their safety because it's very dangerous for the passenger. And I would further explain to the passenger that it's not possible to use the toilet while the seatbelt sign is on and he/she can go to the toilet after the seatbelt sign is off.

| 나의 답변 |

2ND same question

But if he/she still insists on using the toilet, what would you do?

📧 1. I know that there is not enough time to discuss

this while there is turbulence for we cannot afford a moment's delay in regards to his/her safety. So, I would again firmly say to fasten his/her seatbelt and report this to my section leader.

5. What would you say if a passenger is non-compliant by not fastening his/her seat belt before take off?

1. I would request him/her to fasten their seatbelt before take-off for their own safety. I would repeat the request again until he/she responds appropriately and if s/he does follow, I would express my appreciation for his/her compliance. If not, I would inform my section leader to take further action.

---

6. If there is a bomb threat, what would you do?

1. Well if I am in that situation, I would be scared but I would try to be strong and I would make sure all the passengers stayed calm. And of course I would report to chief purser and follow the instructions that I received while training at your company's training school.

In-flight Situation-
Teamwork

  기내상황 질문 중에 teamwork에 관련한 질문은 중요한 질문 유형 중의 하나이다. 승무원직은 독특한 환경과 제한된 시간 내에 모든 승객을 만족시켜야 하는 직업이므로 협조적인 teamwork가 많이 요구된다. 특히, 외국항공사인 경우 only Korean crew-member로서 대다수의 local crew와 일을 해야 하므로, 종종 어떻게 이들과 어울리고 적응을 할 수 있는지에 대한 문제도 물어본다. 이때에도 상황에 따라 감정적으로 행동하지 않고 성숙하게 해결하는 자질을 어필해야 한다.

질문 유형

(About Team work)

1. What is your definition of team work?

1. I think teamwork consists of a group of people
   working together to achieve a common goal. I believe
   one person cannot do everything so the results of

teamwork are better than the results of one person working alone.

2. I think the definition of teamwork is to work together properly in order to achieve the purpose of the team. To accomplish the common goals, the team members have to cooperate with each other while doing one's own responsibility as well. As a team member, I believe I need to respond positively to my member's needs.

| 나의 답변 |

2. Do you prefer to work alone or as a member of a team?

1. I prefer to work as a member of a team because I have realized that in order to meet the team's goals,

one must work together and not alone. When I was a student, I enjoyed working alone because my grades heavily depended on how much work I myself put into it. However, as I have learned, a flight attendant's job has a lot of time restrictions. So, I not only have to work efficiently by myself, but I also have to have good teamwork to reach our goals.

2. I think I am a great team player and prefer to work as a team because of my experiences working together in my school activities and in part-time jobs. Whenever we worked together, we finished our job much more easily and we learned from each other. Through that, I've become more positive and more of an open-minded person.

| 나의 답변 |

3. Tell me about a group assignment or project that you really enjoyed.

1. I recently finished a group project for my graduation. This project was to show a collaboration of creativity, strategy, skills and cooperation. All of my team members brought something unique to the project and together we achieved more than we would have separately. Teamwork is a fantastic thing. It is possible to enjoy more success and a higher level of efficacy while working together. While I like working independently, I really enjoyed this group project and look forward to my next.

| 나의 답변 |

4. How have you handled criticism at your university and work?

📝 1. I think constructive criticism can be very helpful. When I received suggestions regarding my academic and professional work, I was grateful. Although at that time, it might have been difficult to understand why my work wasn't so well received, I tried to listen openly to all the suggestions and used my best judgment to make the changes that I felt would result in the greatest success. Being the best person I can be helps me be the best employee I can be.

| 나의 답변 |

5. Are you a leader or a follower?/ What makes you a leader?

1. I usually take the position of a leader. I think communicating effectively is a fundamental part of having leadership skills and it allows me as a leader, to build a stronger team and deal with the team's concerns more effectively. I believe effective communication can contribute towards better in-flight performance, passenger handling, and interaction with other crewmembers.

| 나의 답변 |

6. If you have a conflict with your senior crewmember because of different opinions, what would you do?

📑 1. At first I would listen actively to my senior crewmember's opinion in order to be aware of what he/she is feeling and thinking. After listening to him/her, I would try to clarify what I think he/she just said by paraphrasing or using a similar approach to avoid any misunderstandings. And then I would take my senior's advice in a positive way and try to get the best result through discussion.

| 나의 답변 |

7. If your section leader asks you to do something, which you feel is not appropriate, what would you do?

1. First I would try to choose the right moment to react to the situation. For example, if something is done in front of the passengers, I should, of course, not question him/her at that time, but if I feel it is important, I might decide to bring it up with my section leader later in the galley. I would try to see the situation from the other person's point of view and consider for example, whether that person is under a lot of pressure or stress and whether that has made him/her communicate more abruptly than usual.

| 나의 답변 |

 온에어 인터뷰

8. During the middle of a long haul flight (e.g. from Hong Kong to London), your crew members suddenly start to talk in Cantonese which you don't understand. (All of your team members are from HONG KONG). All the passengers are sleeping, there is nothing to do, and they are just talking in the galley. In this case what would you do?

1. Well, at first I would kindly ask them to talk in English. But if they are still talking in their own language, even though it might not be easy I would try not to take it personally and I would respect their way of talking. And after the flight I would try to learn their language in order to join in their conversations for the next flight.

| 나의 답변 |

9. During passenger boarding, if you see your boyfriend with another girl getting on board arm in arm down to your duty zone, what would you do?

1. Well, to be honest, it would not be easy to control myself. In this case, I would talk to my section leader about this situation and ask for help to swap my duty position with another colleague. And of course I would try my best to concentrate on my job while on duty and after the flight I would talk to my boyfriend to fix the problem.

1. If you see a passenger take the company's blanket from the cabin, what would you do?

1. I would stop the passenger from taking the blanket because it is the company's property. I would explain to them very politely that it is only for in-flight use and if he/she wants to have it as a souvenir, I would recommend them to buy in-flight duty free items.

| 나의 답변 |

2. If a passenger just pinched your bottom as you were passing by, what would you do?

1. Firstly, I would politely give the passenger the benefit of the doubt, which would be to avoid the assumption that it was harassment, by asking whether he needs any help and I would ask him to press the call button if he needs anything else with a firm tone. But if he keeps touching my body in an obvious manner, I would inform my section leader of this as physical harassment and follow the procedures by the company's regulation.

| 나의 답변 |

온에어 인터뷰

3. If a passenger asks for your phone number, what would you do?

📧 1. If a passenger asks for my phone number I would thank them but I would politely refuse in an indirect way such as that I'm not often at home so it's better if you give me your number. I think I could effectively avoid giving my number to passengers in this way.

| 나의 답변 |

---

4. If a baby keeps crying and a passenger complains of the noise, what would you do?

📧 1. First I would go and check on the baby's condition with its parents. If it is sick I would try my best to comfort it and explain this to the complaining passenger. But if he/she is still complaining I would try to change his/her seat to another seat.

---

5. If children are running in the cabin, what would you do?

1. First I would talk to the children to take their seat with a friendly voice. And I would tell their parents or guardian that the children shouldn't run in the cabin because it is disturbing other passenger's rest and for their own safety. And I would also bring a kid's fun pack for their entertainment to pass the time.

6. What would you say or do if you saw that passengers had been double-seated by the ground staff?

🗨 1. First of all I would apologize about the situation and try to find out which passenger was double-seated. I would ask the passenger who come later to wait for a while until I checked with the ground staff. After I have found a new seat for the passenger, I would guide him to the new seat as soon as possible and help him in arranging his seat. Then I would offer him something to drink etc. for compensation. Once again I would apologize for the inconvenience.

| 나의 답변 |

SEQ
19 # Group discussion &
Debate 1

1) Discussion이란?

일반적인 의미에서 토론이란 강력한 논리전개로 상대방의 발언에서 논리적인 모순을 찾아내고 반박하여, 자신의 주장을 관철시키고 청중의 호의를 얻는 것. 일반적인 토론이 상대의 주장을 반박하고 논리적인 우위성을 입증하여야 한다면, 항공사 디스커션 면접은 Team Work 정신이 있는지, 팀과 잘 어울려 팀의 임무를 수행하는 능력이 있는지, 즉 팀원들과의 의사소통과 조화의 능력을 보는 것임을 이해하여야 한다. 그렇기 때문에 Win-win의 전략으로 가야 하며, 팀의 분위기가 좋으면 팀원 전원이 합격할 수도 있고 팀의 분위기가 안 좋을 때에는 팀원 전원이 탈락하는 경우도 많다.

2) 출제경향

최근에 많은 외국항공사의 면접진행방식이 진화되고 다양화되고 있다.

그 중 많은 외국항공사의 1차 면접의 형태가 디스커션이다.

디스커션을 면접으로 진행 한 항공사는 캐세이퍼시픽 항공, 에띠하드 항공, 에미레이트 항공, 카타르 항공, 싱가포르 항공 등이 있다.

3) 출제방식

6명~20명까지 한팀이 되어 주어진 주제에 대해 자유롭게 토론하거나(자유토론형), 팀 미션이 주어지면 결과를 내어 한 명씩 프리젠테이션 하는 방법이다(결론도출형). 때로는 그룹면접 중간에 일정한 시간과 파트너를 지정해주고(보통은 옆 사람) 파트너를 소개하는, 즉 그룹면접과 디스커션이 접목된 면접형식 등의 변형된 형태로 다양화되고 있는 추세이다.

디스커션은 영어를 유창하게 하여 의견을 논리적으로 말해도 떨어지는 경우가 많고, 발언 수는 적으나 다른 팀원을 배려하며 지지해주는 태도가 좋아 합격하는 경우가 많으므로, 많은 연습과 주의사항을 잘 숙지하여 면접에 임하도록 해야 한다.

4) 그룹 디스커션 시 주의사항

1. Communication Skill

주제를 잘 듣고 그에 맞는 의견을 낸다.

간혹 토론하다가 분위기에 휩쓸려 자기도 모르게 주제에 벗어나는 의견이나 경험담을 이야기하는 경우가 있다.

그럴 경우, 감점의 원인이 되므로 꼭 주제에 맞는 의견만 언급해야 한다.

2. Consideration

의견을 많이 낸다고 좋은 점수를 받는 것은 아니다.

그룹토론의 목적은 영어 실력을 평가하는 것이 아니라 지원자의 성격이나 남들과 얼마나 조화를 잘 이루는지를 보려 하는 것이다.

그러므로 면접관에게 자신을 어필하기 위해 남의 의견을 무시하거나, 남의 말을 끊고 자신의 의견만을 늘어놓는 행동은 불합격의 원인이 된다.

상대방의 의견에 동조해주고 자신의 말과 상대방의 말이 겹쳤다면, you go ahead first나 after you와 같은 말로 상대방을 배려하는 모습을 보여주도록 한다.

외항사 합격자 중 그룹 토론 때 한마디도 못한 경우도 있다.

3. Attention

토론이 진행되는 동안에는 면접관을 보거나 질문하지 않는다.

토론이 시작되면 오직 조원들의 의견에만 집중한다.

면접관과 눈이 마주쳤다거나 면접관에게 질문하는 행동은 토론에 집중하지 않고 있다는 반증.

 온에어 인터뷰

토론이 시작되면 면접관을 의식하지 말고 친구들과 토론을 하고 있다는 생각으로 임하는 것이 좋다.

토론 중에 면접관들은 주위를 돌며 지원자들의 말투, 성격, 외모를 체크한다.

4. Express Empathy

상대방의 의견에 동의와 동조를 하라.

내 의견을 상대방에게 강력히 주장하는 것보다 상대방의 의견을 잘 들어주고, 의견에 동조해주는 것이 중요하다.

지원자의 눈빛에서, 그리고 자연적으로 고개를 끄덕이거나 하는 행동에서 토론에 참여한 태도를 짐작할 수 있다. 이때 팀원들을 바라보는 눈빛이 매우 중요하다.

마치 엄마가 딸을 쳐다보듯 사랑의 눈빛을 쏴 주도록 한다.

| 동의와 동조를 해주는 표현 |

You've got a point there.
I'm with you.
I agree.
I couldn't agree with you more를 사용하면 좋다.

5. Companionship

Win-win 전략으로 가야 한다.

지원자의 팀워크를 볼 수 있는 가장 좋은 면접형태.

속한 그룹의 분위기가 좋을 경우 한 그룹의 80%가 합격하는 경우
가 있는가 하면 1~2명의 합격자만 배출되는 경우도 있다.

경쟁적인 구도보다는 서로 win-win 하려는 태도가 중요.

6. Patience

면접 초보의 돌발행위에 당황하고 위의 태도를 흐트러뜨리지 마라.

이때는 자연스럽게 먼저 하게끔 하고 빨리 분위기를 전환해야 한다.

7. Image

자신의 스타일을 찾아라.

1) 가령 예를 들면, 강하고 적극적인 성격과 경향의 사람이 처음부
터 리드하고 말을 많이 하면, 독선적인 성향으로 보일 수 있다.

반면, 차분하고 온유해 보이는 사람이 대화를 이끌 경우, 리더쉽이
있어 보인다는 느낌을 줄 수 있다.

2) 위의 것은 손의 제스처나 동작에서도 마찬가지이다.

강한 성격의 지원자가 손이나 팔을 강하게 뻗을 경우, strong or
aggressive act라는 평가를 들을 수 있기 때문이다.

Group discussion & Debate 2

Discussion의 종류

1. 자유토론형

6명~20명까지 한팀이 되어 주어진 주제에 대해 자유롭게 토론하는 형태.

이때 면접관이 시간을 정해주고 제한된 시간에 토론하는 경우 time keeper를 정해야 한다. 이때 오프닝 하는 사람이 제안해야 하고, 다른 후보자가 오프닝을 했을 때 제한을 하지 않는다면, 내가 volunteer 하도록 하여 팀 점수가 깎이지 않도록 한다. Time keeper는 매 5분, 그리고 종료 3분 전 알려주어 팀 전체 시간이 오버되지 않고 마무리할 수 있도록 도와야 한다.

| Time keeper의 유용한 표현 |

May I be the time keeper?/ May I check our time?

I'll let you know 3 minutes before end of our discussion.

I'm afraid that we only have 3 minutes left. Why don't we make a conclusion?

We have just 3 minutes to go for further discussion. I think it's better for us to summarize our ideas.

(1) What do you think about international marriage?

(2) What do you want to change the most in your life?

(3) The pros and cons of working in a team.

(4) The duties of cabin crew.

(5) The cultural differences between Korean & any other foreign countries.

(6) What do you know about our Airline?

(7) What do you think of women smoker?

(8) What would you do if you suddenly have one billion dollars?

(9) Do you think that sports develop good character?

(11) Which country would you like to go first after becoming a flight attendant?

(12) If you got a chance to born again what gender would you choose?

(13) If your boyfriend cheated on you with your girl friend what would you do?

(14) If you have a power that can change anything, what would you do?

(15) If you were the ingredient of a salad, what would you like to be?

(16) The duties of cabin crew.

영어로 자유롭게 자신의 의견을 말하는 데 다소 자신이 없거나 소극적인 경향의 후보자는 opening을 적극적으로 하도록 한다. 가장 첫 발언인 만큼 인상 깊게 보일 수 있으므로 후반부에 발언 양이 적다 하더라도 opening을 할 경우 보완될 수 있다. Opening을 하는 사람은 팀원 전체를 대화에 끌어들이는, 즉 팀원을 engaging 하는 역할이므로 부드럽고 친절하지만 자신감 있게 주도한다. 반대로 말이 많거나 주도적인 성향이 강한 사람, 그리고 영어실력이 원어민 수준이라고 여겨지는 후보자들은 가급적 오프닝을 피하고 support 하는 경향으로 가는 것이 유리하다.

| 순 서 |

1. 인사

(Hello everyone. Good morning 이때 주의사항: hello guys(x) guys는 쓰지 않도록 한다.)

2. 이름소개

My name is Eun hae Lee. You can call me Grace.

3. Ice break(날씨/칭찬)

It's very sunny day today. I hope we have great discussion together.

I am very glad to see such beautiful ladies and nice gentleman here today.

I am honored to have this wonderful ladies and gentleman today.

4. 토론 주제언급(시간제한 있을 시 time keeper 제안)

Today's topic is…

5. 첫 발언 제안

Shall we start our discussion?

Anybody wants to say first?

6. 5초간 아무도 발언 하지 않을 경우

본인이 발언을 해도 되는지 물어본다. 그리고 발언시작. Opening 한 사람은 첫 발언 주의.

| 유용한 표현 |

If you don't mind, may I go first?

Do you mind if I start first?

If nobody wants to talk, may I do first?

2. 결론도출형

  주어진 시간에 팀에게 미션이 주어지면 팀의 의견을 모아 문제에 맞게 결론을 내리고, 때에 따라 한 명씩 Presentation 하는 방식이다. Presentation 할 때에는 개인에게 할당된 시간(1~2분)만큼만 말하도록 하고 시간을 초과하지 않도록 주의해야 한다. team-work spirit을 보는 것이기 때문에 내가 낸 의견이라 할지라도 발표할 때에는 반드시 주어를 we, 또는 our team 이런 형식으로 발표해야 한다.

| 기출질문 예 |

(1) Discuss a pros and cons about following travel methods.

    (Cruise, Backpacker, Group travel)

(2) Discuss a 1 day Trip for interviewer.

(3) The ship is sinking and you can rescue only 5 passengers among 11 survivors.

    Make the list of the 5people.

(4) You are about to open a restaurant in Seoul and your team have to choose the location, interior decoration, the menu and the shop name, etc.

(5) One of the passenger is a house keeper an goes back to her hometown. She is poor, tired and thirsty. Decide 10

special services for her.

(6) Say 3 nationality you don't want to stay together as a roommate except China, Japan, Korea.

(7) Make a birthday party for your deaf friend.

(8) Think of 5 items you would take to survive for a year on a tropical island.

(9) What are 3 important things for friendship?

(10) How can you care for Johnny who is 8 years old and travels to South Africa if you are a flight attendant?

3. 파트너 소개

주의사항: 시선 처리 주의. 청중이 무리를 이루는 그룹 단위로 시선을 천천히, 도장을 찍듯이 눌러주며 시선을 옮겨야 한다. 파트너가 나를 소개할 때, 또는 내가 파트너를 소개할 때 너무 파트너만 바라보지 않도록 주의하여야 한다.

(1) 주제 없는 파트너 소개

| 순 서 |

1. Ice break(인사/간단한 자기 이름소개)

EX: Good morning everyone! It's very nice meeting you all. My name is OOO.

And today, I am very glad to introduce my gorgeous partner.

2. 파트너 이름(나이)

Her name is Eun hae Lee

3. 학교, 전공/하는 일

She is a student majoring in Education at ONAIR University.

Now, she works for a trading company.

4. 특이사항(다른 사람과 구별되는 흥미를 끌만한 것)

She lived in America for 5 years. 그녀는 미국에 5년간 살았었다.

She was once a promising actress. 그녀는 한때 촉망받는 신인 배우였다.

5. The reason why s/he wants to be a flight attendant. (파트너가 승무원이 되고자 하는 이유)

6. Closing(반드시 파트너와 win-win의 의지를 보여주어야 한다- 칭찬)

Ex: Even though it wasn't as long to know each other, I had such a great time with my partner000 and even I found out that she is very qualified and nice person to be a F/A.

I hope I could fly with her in the near future at Emirates Airlines. Thank you.

(2) 주제 있는 파트너 소개

1. Opening(인사/간단한 자기 이름소개/Ice break)

Ex: Good morning everyone! It's very nice meeting you all. My name is 000.

And today, I'm very happy to introduce about my partner's favorite food.

2. 파트너 이름

Her name is Eun hae Lee

3. 학교, 전공/하는 일

She is a student majoring in Education at ONAIR University.

4. 주제(ex: favorite food)

My partner's favorite food is...

5. Closing(win-win 전략으로 파트너 칭찬과 함께 마무리)

Ex: Even though it wasn't as long to know each other, I had such a great time with my partner000 and even I found out that she is very qualified and nice person to be a F/A.

I hope I could fly with her in the near future at Emirates Airlines. Thank you.

4. Debate

　찬성과 반대로 나뉘어 토론하는 방식. 이때 원하는 파트를 선택할 수 없으며 면접관이 지정해주는 곳에 앉아야 한다. 따라서 내가 토론하는 주제에 대해 찬성의 의견을 갖고 있어도 반대쪽에 있거나 반대의 의견을 갖고 있어도 찬성 쪽에 있는 경우가 있을 수 있다. Debate에서는 상대방이 내 의견에 반복적으로 반대 의견을 제시해도 감정적으로 연루되지 않고 끝까지 침착함을 잃지 않는 것이 중요한 point라고 볼 수 있다. 집요하게 내 의견에 반대하는 사람이 있다면, 그것을 주장하는 다른 근거를 제시하여 빠져나오도록 해야 한다.

| 기출질문 예 |

(1) Eating dog-meat.

(2) Death penalty.

(3) Cohabitation before marriage.

(4) Using animals for scientific experiments.

(5) Teenagers should not be allowed to use SNS to communicate with others.

(6) Plastic surgery

5. 기타 유용한 표현

(1) 의견을 제시할 때

As for my opinion 제 의견으로는

In my opinion… 제 의견으로는

The way I see it… 제가 보기에는(제 의견으로는)

From my point of view… ???

What I think is that 저는 ~라고 생각합니다.

Let me put it this way. 제가 이렇게 한번 말해보죠.

Let me put it in another way. 다른 식으로 이야기해보죠.

Let me put it a different way. 다른 식으로 말해보죠.

(2) 동의할 때

I agree with your idea. 저도 그렇게 생각합니다.

I agree with your suggestion 100 percent. 당신의 의견에 100%찬성입니다.

I support your opinion. 당신의 의견에 동의합니다.

I think I'm with you on this one. 당신의 의견에 동의합니다.

I am with you on that point. 나는 그 점에 있어서 당신과 동일한 생각입니다.

I am all for it. 저는 그것에 대찬성입니다.

I have the same thoughts as you. 저도 같은 생각입니다.

That makes sense to me. ???

(3) 다른 의견 제시 할 때

I think I have a different opinion on that. 전 그 점에 대해서는 의견이 다릅니다.

I see things differently. 제 생각은 좀 다릅니다.

I see myself differently ???

I agree with you to some extent, but~ 어느 정도는 동의합니다만

I partly agree with your point but 부분적으로 ~에 동의합니다만

You've got a point there, but~ 그 말씀은 맞지만

I think on this one I am going to have to disagree with you. 이 문제에 대해 저는 당신에게 반대해야 할 것 같습니다.

(4) 질문할 때

What do you think about…? ~에 대해 어떻게 생각하십니까?

How about…? ~는 어떻습니까?

What about…? ???

(5) 끝말

I've enjoyed talking with you all and I hope to see you again soon.

It's been a great time with you and I hope we can see each other soon.

| Airline Terminologies |

1. Air bridge

A linking passageway between the airport terminal and the aircraft.

2. Apron

An area in front of an aircraft hangar used for parking aircraft.

3. Airborne

When an aircraft is in the air and flying.

4. Altitude

Height above sea level.

5. Approach

The final stage of a flight when an aircraft is coming close to the runway for landing.

6. Ascend

When an aircraft climbs to a higher altitude after take-off.

7. Belly

The lower or underneath part of an aircraft's body.

8. Bulkhead

A wall or partition that divides the passenger, cabin into separate sections.

9. Cruise

To fly at a sustained altitude and at a relatively constant speed.

10. Descend

When an aircraft flies from a higher to a lower altitude in preparation for landing.

11. Fuselage

The body of an aircraft, excluding the wings, tail and engines.

12. Flight Deck

The area at the front of the aircraft where the pilot works and where all the controls are.

13. Galley

The section of the aircraft used for storing and preparing food and beverages.

14. Headwind

Wind coming from the opposite direction in which the aircraft is flying. It hinders the aircraft and makes the flight longer.

15. Hangar

A large building in which aircraft are kept.

16. Main Gear

The landing gear under the belly of an aircraft.

17. Nose Gear

The landing gear under the nose of an aircraft.

18. Runway

A long narrow strip of ground with a hard level surface which is used by aircraft when they are taking off and landing.

19. Tailwind

The opposite of headwind.

20. Take-off

When an aircraft leaves the ground.

21. Taxi

When an aircraft moves on the ground under its own power.

22. Turbulence

Irregular and bumpy movement of an aircraft normally due to bad weather conditions.

| 참고 서적 |

케세이 퍼시픽 항공(1996), Induction Training Course, Inflight Service Training Center

유정선(2013), 승무원 되는 항공 인터뷰 영어, 한올출판사.

이은영, 김민수(2009), 항공 승무원 인터뷰, 새로미.

Myeong-Hee Seong, Katie Mae Klemsen(2011), Interview English, 백산출판사.

박혜정, Scott J.Covey(2008), English Interview for Stewardesses, 백산출판사.

최성희(2014), 승무원영어면접 Answer, 생각나눔

· ONAIR INTERVIEW ·

www.onairinterview.com

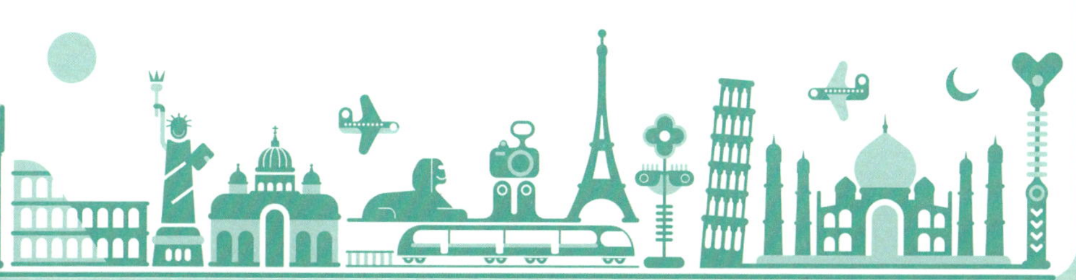

온에어인터뷰

펴 낸 날 2015년 5월 26일

지 은 이 김원희
펴 낸 이 최지숙
편집주간 이기성
편집팀장 이윤숙
기획편집 윤은지, 김송진, 주민경, 박경진
표지디자인 윤은지
책임마케팅 임경수
감　　수 Faith Huh
펴 낸 곳 도서출판 생각나눔
출판등록 제 2008-000008호
주　　소 서울 마포구 동교로 18길 41, 한경빌딩 2층
전　　화 02-325-5100
팩　　스 02-325-5101
홈페이지 www.생각나눔.kr
이 메 일 webmaster@think-book.com

• 책값은 표지 뒷면에 표기되어 있습니다.
  ISBN 978-89-6489-391-3   13740

• 이 도서의 국립중앙도서관 출판 시 도서목록(CIP)은 서지정보유통지원시스템 홈페이지
  (http://seoji.nl.go.kr)와 국가자료공동목록시스템(http://www.nl.go.kr/kolisnet)에서
  이용하실 수 있습니다(CIP제어번호: CIP2015013500).